To Mark

Enjoy

From John. 1996.

RAILWAY WALKS

From 1 April 1996, local authority boundaries in Scotland will change.
For up-to-date information, contact the relevant regional council
or the Scottish Office:

Dumfries & Galloway (01387) 61234
Borders (01835) 823301
Strathclyde (0141) 204 2900
Lothian (0131) 229 9292
Central (01786) 442000
Fife (01592) 754411
Scottish Office, Edinburgh (0131) 556 8400

This edition published in 1995 by
Marshall Cavendish Books, London
(a division of Marshall Cavendish Partworks Ltd)

Copyright © Marshall Cavendish 1995

ISBN 1 85435 835 9

British Library Cataloguing in Publication Data:
A catalogue record for this book is available from the British Library

Printed and bound in Spain

Some of this material has previously appeared in the Marshall Cavendish partwork OUT & ABOUT

CONTENTS

6 Foreword

8 Introduction

SCOTLAND
15 **1** Beside the Deeside

THE NORTH
19 **2** The Riches of Ravenglass • *21* **3** Following the River Ribble
23 **4** Steaming Across the Moors • *27* **5** By Clifftop and Golden Line
29 **6** The Bronte Moors • *33* **7** Thurstaston Hill

CENTRAL ENGLAND
35 **8** Mills and Kilns • *39* **9** Looking High and Low

THE EAST
43 **10** Across Lindsey Marsh • *47* **11** Eight Sails to the Wind • *51* **12** Steaming to Thursford
53 **13** Norfolk Nature Walk • *57* **14** Secret Valley

THE SOUTH EAST
59 **15** The Line to Ally Pally • *63* **16** The Castle on the Rother
65 **17** Horses and Courses

THE SOUTH WEST
69 **18** Around Osmington • *73* **19** The Avon Navigation • *77* **20** Deepest Devon
79 **21** The Red Cliffs and the Railway • *81* **22** The Camel Trail

WALES
83 **23** The Slopes of Snowdon • *85* **24** Welshpool
89 **25** Cwm Rheidol • *93* **26** North of Aberystwyth

95 Index

Foreword

There can be few sights more impressive than a train in full steam chugging across a viaduct over a lush green valley. Sadly, this is a sight rarely to be seen today. It is possible, however, to walk the routes of these fiery leviathans through some of the most panoramic countryside in Great Britain and to appreciate the monumental achievements of the early railwaymen, the men of vision, the engineers and the thousands of migrant labourers, the navvies.

The earliest records of what we have come to term a railway system date from the early 1600s when Henry Beaumont, colliery owner and engineer, laid down two miles of wooden track from the pithead of his colliery at Wollaton near Nottingham. By the end of the eighteenth century, these wagon-ways, as they came to be called, were becoming ever more sophisticated. Following the development of iron-making, pioneered by the Darbys of Coalbrookdale, the tracks were improved by laying a metal strip over the wood until eventually the entire track was made of metal. Once again, the colliery districts were at the forefront of experimentation. In 1776, mining engineer John Curr introduced the metal plateway into the underground mines which held the wagons to the track and made an enormous difference to the working lives of the young boys and girls who had previously moved the coal from the face in baskets on their backs.

STEAM POWER

British engineers also led they way in the development of the invention that would combine with the railway to create a whole new transport system: the steam engine. Although James Watt, fearful of the effects of using high-pressure steam, refused to develop his atmospheric pressure engine, it was quickly appreciated that a piston working in two directions within a closed cylinder could be used, in conjunction with a crank, to turn a wheel. This could in turn be used to work machinery in a factory, to turn the paddle wheels of a boat, or to turn the wheels of a vehicle on land.

GOODS TRAINS

When Watt's patent expired in 1800 Richard Trevithick began work using high-pressure steam, and in 1801 his road engine successfully transported a party of local dignitaries up a hill near Camborne. He was unable, however, to generate much interest in the project and turned his attention to the tramways in use in the collieries. Again, although his engine was a success, the railway failed as the cast-iron rails cracked under the weight of the engine. It seemed as though the use of steam locomotives in the collieries was doomed as lighter engines could not carry the heavy loads required. In 1808, John Blenkinsop, owner of a colliery near Leeds, approached a local engineer, Matthew Murray, who solved the problem by designing the rack-and-pinion engine. Using traction, a five-ton engine could now haul 90 tons without damage to the track. His Middleton Colliery Railway was a triumph and by 1812 a regular service was in operation. In 1813 George

Stephenson travelled from Tyneside to see for himself and built his own locomotive in 1814 for the Killingworth colliery.

THE GOLDEN AGE OF STEAM

Improvements continued for the next decade until, in 1825, the world's first public railway built specifically to carry passengers and freight by steam locomotive, the Stockton & Darlington Railway, was opened. The official invitation to the opening ceremony on 27 September read that "A superior locomotive, of the most superior construction, will be employed with a train of convenient carriages, for the conveyance of the proprietors and strangers." The superior locomotive was none other than George Stephenson's famous engine, Locomotion.

The Stockton & Darlington Railway was used mainly for the carriage of coal and other goods, employing both steam locomotives and horses for traction. In another five years, the first full passenger-carrying railway, solely dependent on steam locomotives – the Liverpool & Manchester Railway – became fully operational. Before long, another main route, the London & Birmingham Railway, was added to the network, swiftly followed by Brunel's Great Western Railway.

This was the beginning of the Golden Age of steam. For over one hundred years, Great Britain was criss-crossed by 11,000 miles of track, and over 8,000 towns and villages boasted a station. A typical example surviving today is Ballater station on the now-redundant Deeside Railway, famous in the nineteenth century for transporting Queen Victoria and a distinguished array of visitors, including members of the European aristocracy and heads of state, to Balmoral.

Given that the accepted track incline was generally 1 in 100, the major railway routes were constructed on a principal known as 'cut and fill', cutting through rising ground and using the excavated material to build up embankments to cross the next valley. And where the hills and vales of the British countryside proved too much for cut and fill, the railway engineers built viaducts and tunnels. One of the most scenic routes in Britain, the 21-mile Scarborough–Whitby railway nicknamed the Golden Line, ran over 60 bridges, two viaducts and many cuttings and embankments, as well as through two tunnels. When walking these deserted railway lines today, it is sobering to remember that every mile of the route was created by human hand. There were no diggers, cranes and rollers – just picks, shovels and wheelbarrows.

IN DECLINE

The railways prospered until they fell into decline after World War I. Then a combination of events led to a major rethink and the now infamous Beeching Report. At a stroke, 8,000 miles of track were lost. Although in many cases the sleepers have been pulled up and the buildings allowed to fall into disrepair, our imaginations can supply the missing details. Stand beneath a smoke-blackened tunnel or at the top of a wind-swept embankment and it is not hard to feel the enveloping steam or hear the driver's whistle as the train thunders past.

Introduction to
RAILWAY WALKS

W alking has become one of the most popular pastimes in Britain. To enjoy walking, you don't need any special skills, you don't have to follow rules or join expensive clubs, and you don't need any special equipment – though a pair of walking boots is a good idea! It is an easy way of relaxing and getting some exercise, and of enjoying nature and the changing seasons.

RAILWAY WALKS *will give you ideas for walks in your own neighbourhood and in other areas of Britain. All the walks are devised to appeal to railway enthusiasts and general walkers alike, and range in length from about 2 to 9 miles (3.25 to 14.5 km) and in difficulty from very easy to mildly strenuous. Whether circular or linear, the walks have been planned so that you will always be able to get back to your starting point.*

THE WALKS

Devised by experts and tested for accuracy, each walk is accompanied by clear instructions and an enlarged section of an Ordnance Survey map. The flavour of the walk and highlights to look out for are described in the introductory text. Feature boxes provide extra insight into items of local historical and environmental interest.

FACT FILE

The fact file gives at-a-glance information about each walk to help you make your selection.

✳	**general location**
os	**map reference for Ordnance Survey map with grid reference for starting point**
	length of the walk in miles and kilometres
	miles 0 1 2 3 4 5 6 7 8 9
	kms 0 1 2 3 4 5 6 7 8 9 10 11 12 13 14 15
◔	**time needed if walking at an average speed**
▬	**character of the walk: easy/easy with strenuous parts/mildly strenuous; hills to be climbed and muddy or dangerous areas are pointed out**
P	**parking facilities near the start of the walk**
T	**public transport information**
🛢	**facilities for refreshment, including pubs serving lunchtime meals, restaurants, tea rooms and picnic areas**
WC	**location of tolets**
⌒	**historic sites**

ABOVE: *Railways gradually took over from inland waterways as the preferred system of transport for both goods and passengers. Colourful narrowboats are still an attractive feature of Britain's coutryside.*

LOCAL HISTORY

RAILWAY WALKS relates the history of Britain's railways; how the industrial revolution combined with developments in engineering to produce the steam age. It also retells ancient legends, points out architectural details and famous residents, past and present, explains traditional crafts, and uncovers the secrets behind an ever-changing landscape.

DISCOVER NATURE

One of the greatest pleasures of going for a walk is the sense of being close to nature. On these walks, you can feel the wind, smell the pine trees, hear the birds and see the beauty of the countryside, as well as discover Britain's railway heritage.

You will become more aware of the seasons – the beginning of new life in the forests and fields, the bluebell carpets in spring woodlands, the dazzling beauty of rhododendron bushes in early summer, the swaying cornfields of summer, and the golden colours of leaves in autumn. RAILWAY WALKS tells you what to look out for and where to find it.

ORDNANCE SURVEY MAPS

All the walks in the RAILWAY WALKS are illustrated on large-scale, full-colour maps supplied by the Ordnance Survey which is justifiably proud of its worldwide reputation for excellence and accuracy. For extra clarity, the maps have been enlarged to a scale of 1:21,120 (3 inches to 1 mile).

The route for each walk is marked clearly on the map, together with numbered stages that relate to the walk directions and letters noting points of interest that are described in detail in the text.

RIGHTS OF WAY

Throughout the countryside there is a network of paths and byways. Most are designated 'rights of way': footpaths, open only to people on foot, and

RIGHT: *The picturesque village of Widecombe in the heart of Dartmoor makes a beautiful setting for the annual fair.*

BELOW: *Brown hares boxing in spring.*

bridleways, open to people on foot, horseback or bicycle. These paths can be identified on Ordnance Survey maps and verified, in cases of dispute, by the relevant local authority.

THE LAW OF TRESPASS

If you find a public right of way barred to you, you may remove the obstruction or take a short detour around it. However, in England and Wales, if you stray from the footpath you are trespassing and could be sued in a civil court for damages. In Scotland, rights of way are not recorded on definitive maps, nor is there a law of trespass. Although you may cross mountain and moorland paths,

THE COUNTRY CODE

- **Enjoy the countryside, and respect its life and work**

- **Always guard against risk of fire**

- **Fasten all gates**

- **Keep your dogs under close control**

- **Keep to public footpaths across farmland**

- **Use gates and stiles to cross fences, hedges and walls**

- **Leave livestock, crops and machinery alone**

- **Take your litter home**

- **Help to keep all water clean**

- **Protect wildlife, plants and trees**

- **Take special care on country roads**

- **Make no unnecessary noise**

landowners are permitted to impose restrictions on access, which should be obeyed.

ABOVE RIGHT: *Carelessness with cigarettes, matches or camp fires can be devastating in a forest, especially during a period of drought.*

COMMONS AND PARKS

Walkers are generally able to wander freely on most commons and beaches in England and Wales. There are also country parks, set up by local authorities for public recreation – parkland, woodland, heath or farmland.

Most regions of great scenic beauty in England and Wales are designated National Parks or Areas of Outstanding Natural Beauty (AONB). In Scotland, they are known as National Scenic Areas (NSAs)

or AONBs. Most of this land is privately owned and there is no right of public access although local authorities may have negotiated access agreements.

CONSERVATION

National park, AONB or NSA status is intended to protect the landscape, guarding against unsuitable development while encouraging enjoyment of its beauty. Nature reserves are areas which are set aside for conservation. Although some offer public access, most require permission to enter.

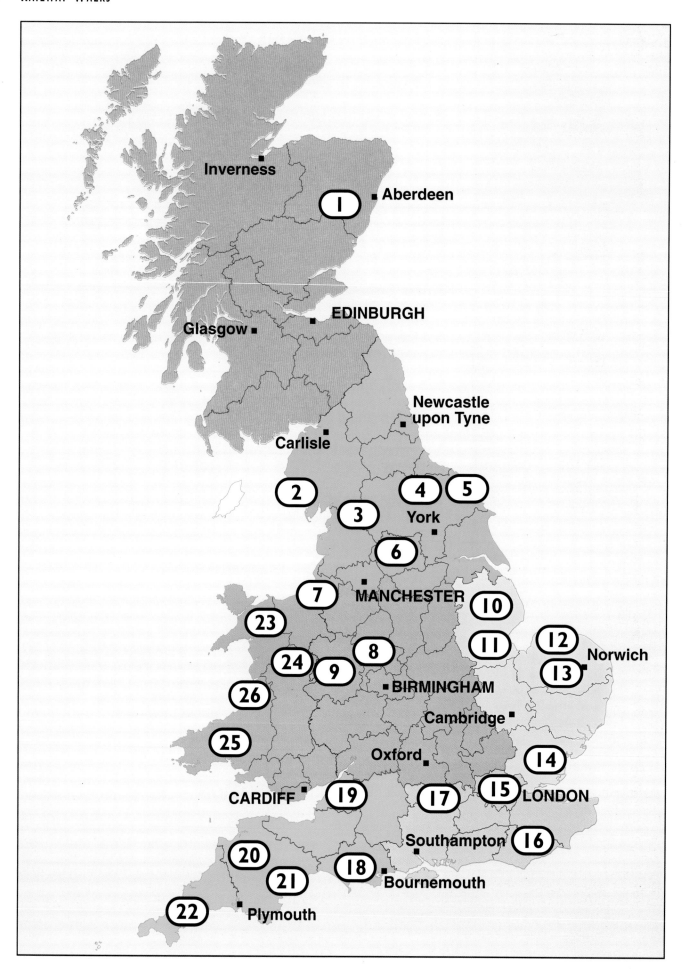

Railway Walks

All the walks featured in this book are plotted and numbered on the map opposite and listed in the box below.

1 Beside the Deeside
2 The Riches of Ravenglass
3 Following the River Ribble
4 Steaming Across the Moors
5 By Clifftop and Golden Line
6 The Brontë Moors
7 Thurstaston Hill
8 Mill and Kilns
9 Looking High and Low

10 Across Lindsey Marsh
11 Eight Sails to the Wind
12 Steaming to Thursford
13 Norfolk Nature Walk
14 Secret Valley
15 The Line to Ally Pally
16 The Castle on the Rother
17 Horses and Courses
18 Around Osmington

19 The Avon Navigation
20 Deepest Devon
21 The Red Cliffs and the Railway
22 The Camel Trail
23 The Slopes of Snowdon
24 Welshpool
25 Cwm Rheidol
26 North of Aberystwyth

*F*aster than fairies, faster than witches,
Bridges and houses, hedges and ditches;
And charging along like troops in a battle,
All through the meadows the horses and cattle:
All of the sights of the hill and the plain
Fly as thick as driving rain;
And ever again, in the wink of any eye,
Painted stations whistle by.

From a Railway Carriage
Robert Louis Stevenson

USING MAPS

Although RAILWAY WALKS gives you all the information you need, it is useful to have some basic map skills.

A large-scale map is the answer to identifying where you are. Britain is fortunate in having the best mapping agency in the world, the Ordnance Survey, which produces high-quality maps, the most popular being the 1:50,000 Landranger series. However, the most useful for walkers are the 1:25,000 Pathfinder, Explorer and Outdoor Leisure maps.

THE LIE OF THE LAND

A map provides more than just a bird's eye view of the land, it also conveys information about the terrain. It distinguishes between footpaths and bridleways and shows boundaries.

Symbols are used to identify a variety of landmarks such as churches, stations, castles and caves. The shape of the land is indicated by contour lines. Each line represents land at a specific height so it is possible to read the gradient from the spacing of the lines.

GRID REFERENCES

All Ordnance Survey maps are overprinted with a framework of squares known as the National Grid. This is a reference system which, by breaking the country down into squares, allows you to pinpoint any place in the country and give it a unique reference number; very useful when making rendezvous arrangements. On OS Landranger, Pathfinder and Outdoor Leisure maps it is possible to give a reference to an accuarcy of 100 metres. Grid squares on these maps cover an area of 1 km x 1 km on the ground.

GIVING A GRID REFERENCE

Blenheim Palace in Oxfordshire has a grid reference of **SP 441 161**. This is constructed as follows:

SP These letters identify the 100 km grid square in which Blenheim Palace lies. These squares form the basis of the National Grid. Information on the

100 km square covering a particular map is always given in the map key.

441 161 This six figure reference locates the position of Blenheim Palace to 100 metres in the 100 km grid square.

44 This part of the reference is the number of the grid line which forms the western (left-hand) boundary of the 1 km grid square in which Blenheim Palace appears. This number is printed in the top and bottom margins of the relevant OS map (Pathfinder 1092 in this case).

16 This part of the reference is the number of the grid line which forms the southern (lower) boundary of the 1 km grid square in which Blenheim Palace appears. This number is printed in the left- and right-hand margins of the relevant OS map (Pathfinder 1092).

These two numbers together (SP 4416) locate the bottom left-hand corner of

the 1 km grid square in which Blenheim Palace appears. The remaining figures in the reference **441 161** pinpoint the position within that square by dividing its western boundary lines into tenths and estimating on which imaginary tenths line Blenheim Palace lies.

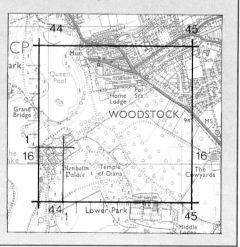

Explore the environs of the town nearest to Balmoral Castle

When Queen Victoria stepped down from the train at Ballater in 1853, she set the royal seal of approval on a town that still basks in her reflected glory. Many of the large Victorian houses on the tree-lined streets were obviously inspired by nearby Balmoral, and no less than eight of the town's shops display the royal warrant.

Victoria's arrival heralded a new awareness of the unspoilt beauty at the heart of royal Deeside. Embraced by rugged mountains, which almost overwhelm the town, Ballater nestles in a deep valley, where the pine-clad banks of the Dee sweep in a graceful curve along the silver length of the river.

FACT FILE

* Ballater, 35 miles (56km) west of Aberdeen, on the A93

⌖ Pathfinder 256 (NO 29/39), grid reference NO 369957

miles 0 1 2 3 4 5 6 7 8 9 10 miles
kms 0 1 2 3 4 5 6 7 8 9 10 11 12 13 14 15 kms

◔ Allow 2½ hours

▬ One steep, rocky climb to the summit of Craigendarroch, otherwise mostly level riverside paths and tarmac roads

P Plentiful in Ballater

🍴 Several shops, pubs and restaurants in Ballater

WC In the car park at the start

I Tourist information in Ballater, open April-end October, Tel. (013397) 55306

▲*The delightful, sparkling waters of the River Dee wind between lightly wooded banks, where the pine beauty moth (inset), with its delicately shaded wings, can be seen flying in April.*

Until the latter half of the 18th century, Ballater was nothing more than brooding, desolate moorland. Somewhat ironically, this royal town owes its existence to a staunch Jacobite, who narrowly escaped execution following his involvement in the Battle of Culloden.

DREAM SPA

Colonel Francis Farquharson, Laird of Monaltrie, returned to his homeland after a 20-year exile and learned of the remarkable healing properties of the waters at nearby Pannanich, where, in 1760, an elderly woman was miraculously cured of scrofula by bathing her sores and bandages in a bog to

THE WALK

BALLATER – BRIDGE OF GAIRN

The walk begins from the car park behind Glenmuick Church in Ballater's main square.

▶ **1** Head to the front of the church. Turn left along the main road, passing the station **A**. Over the bridge, continue ahead to Craigendarroch Walk.

▶ **2** Turn right. After 100 yards (90m), bear right onto a footpath signposted 'To Top & Round'. Continue to a T-junction with a broad path. Turn left. Continue uphill, then turn sharp left at a signpost in a tree. At a fork by a seat, bear left, uphill (signposted 'To Top'). Bear right at a fork to the cairn and the viewpoint at the summit of Craigendarroch **B**. Return to the seat and turn left, signposted 'Round'. Follow the woodland path for almost a mile (1.6km), through the Pass of Ballater **C**, to the first junction of paths after a stone wall. Near a seat, turn right, downhill, to the main road.

▶ **3** Turn right. At the post office at Bridge of Gairn, turn left into the lane opposite. Continue walking on the farm road, to Glengairn Church **D**. Retrace your steps and turn right at a junction behind the farm building.

▶ **4** Follow the track past houses onto a footpath. Take the first right after the footbridge, onto a narrow path to the River Dee **E**. Bear left and follow the riverside path through a picnic area and a golf course to a caravan park.

▶ **5** Turn left onto a path between fences, then continue on a road. At the crossroads, turn right into Victoria Road. Turn left after the Loirston Hotel, then second right. Turn left to return to the car park.

JASON SMALLEY

◀ *The walk begins not far from Glenmuick Church, whose spire soars gracefully above the town of Ballater.*

which she was guided by dreams.

The enterprising laird soon established a lodge on the site of the well, the beginnings of a spa town known as 'Baile challater', town of the wooden stream. With the help of a local luminary, Sandy Dunn, he laid out a grid of streets and building plots on the black moor.

Completed in 1808, the remote spa town thrived. Tourists began to flock to Deeside, much to the alarm of Dr Joseph Robertson, an Aberdeen historian and journalist, who bemoaned the influx of incomers and proclaimed that the glens would be 'desolated by cockneys and other horrid reptiles'.

The building of the Deeside Railway attracted even more visitors. The spruce little Station Square **A** became the scene of frequent fashionable arrivals and departures, as members of the European aristocracy, as well as heads of state and eminent lords and ladies, made their way to the Balmoral Estate. The Shah of Persia came here, and Tsar Nicholas II of Russia arrived in September 1896 to be hailed by 100 men of the Black Watch, before setting off with his retinue in a torchlight procession of five imperial carriages.

In 1856, plans were mooted to extend the line to Braemar. These were vetoed by the Queen, who objected to it running so close to her 'dear paradise' of Balmoral. Ballater's beautifully preserved station remained the end of the line.

ANCIENT OAKS

Craigendarroch **B**, north of the town, presents a steep climb through a chiselled dome of red granite crags, deeply wooded with oak, pine, birch and aspen. The name means 'hills of the oaks', and the magnificent specimens that remain have endured several devastating gales and two

◀The projecting porch on the front of the old, wood-built station building at Ballater, smartly painted in red and white, has protected the heads of many important and famous personages from the elements, not least of whom was Queen Victoria.

▼The route climbs to the heather-clad summit of Craigendarroch, which offers a splendid view of the wide Dee Valley.

woodland fires since World War II.

The view from the summit is awe-inspiring. Ballater spreads out as a model village far below. The Royal Bridge, opened by Victoria in 1885 to link the town with the south Deeside road, is the fourth attempt to span the Dee here. The previous bridges were all swept away by the river when it was in full spate.

Thomas Telford built the most elegant structure, whose five graceful arches stood till the great flood of August 1829, when they became so jammed with fallen trees, drowned cattle, sheep, pigs and poultry, and the water was dammed to such a great height, that a thunderous crack shook the bridge's very foundations, and the whole thing collapsed into the deluge.

The narrow opening of Glen Muick is to the right. When Victoria first visited Balmoral, in 1848, she fell in love with the glen, and wrote in her journal that the name meant 'darkness' or 'sorrow'. This was wishful thinking; Glen Muick means 'Valley of the Pigs', and owes its name to the wild boars that roamed the ancient Caledonian forests.

DARK LOCHNAGAR

Further off to the right are the peaks of Balmoral deer forest. The highest is the dramatic, 3,700-foot-high (1,128-m) ridge of Lochnagar, immortalized by Byron as 'dark Lochnagar', and once climbed by Queen Victoria. The area is now a nature reserve run by the Scottish Wildlife Trust and Balmoral Estate.

Round the northern slopes of Craigendarroch is the Pass of Ballater ❶, a deep, narrow gorge, which was once the only entrance to the Braemar highlands. Peregrine falcons, sparrowhawks and buzzards hunt through the precipitous corries, and the pass is a source of semi-precious stones — garnets, topaz and a peat-coloured quartz called cairngorm. Some of these stones are huge; one specimen found locally measured more than 2 feet (60cm) in length. Along the edge of the pass, the white heads of cotton-grass dance among the masses of purple heather.

You descend again into the valley of the Dee. Near the ruined shell of Glengairn Church ❶ is St Mungo's Well, dedicated to the patron saint of Glasgow. An annual fair was held in his honour on the nearby hillside of Abergairn. The people of Gairn were an isolated community, and prey to superstition; there was a widespread belief that those who failed to attend the Feast of St Mungo, held on the longest day of summer, would not live to see the following year.

The church was last used for public worship in 1799. It was left to crumble amid the stones of its graveyard, mute witnesses to the

▼The climb to the top of the hill is on a steep, rocky path, but the wild flowers and the woodland are delightful.

ALL PHOTOS: JASON SMALLEY

At Her Majesty's Convenience

The luxurious red mahogany toilet built for the use of Queen Victoria at the now-closed Ballater Station has been faithfully reassembled at the town's Loirston Hotel.

Despite the Deeside Railway's illustrious association with Queen Victoria, she was a poor traveller; her kilted Highland escort, John Brown, once strode along the platform to relay her Majesty's displeasure to the driver — the train was 'shaking like the devil'.

However, the Queen used the line for almost half a century. When Ballater's handsome new station was built, it incorporated a royal waiting room and toilet, and was the only station in Scotland to possess such an impressive facility.

In February 1966, the last passenger train left the deserted platform, followed in December by the final freight train. It was the end of the line for the Deeside Railway, but not for the royal waiting room.

After a decent interval, the contents were offered for tender and purchased by Ballater's Loirston Hotel. Now, a train of visitors trek through the hotel foyer en route to visit this delightfully preserved fragment of Victoriana. The famous toilet and washbasin are in full working order, though pilgrims invariably feel it would be somewhat sacrilegious to actually use such historic receptacles. Fortunately, the proprietors have sufficient taste to forgo the obvious royal epithet, 'Queen Victoria sat here'.

◀ *The impressive, dark and brooding ridge of Lochnagar, which has inspired works from writers as diverse as Lord Byron and Prince Charles.*

▶ *This shop on Golf Road in Ballater, with its warrants on display outside, is one of many in the town to proudly boast a royal seal of approval.*

ALL PHOTOS: JASON SMALLEY

lives of those who once created a thriving community here. Inside the roofless church, the stump of a mature ash, crudely fashioned into a giant chair, puts out new suckers.

The return to Ballater follows the the banks of the impetuous River Dee **E**, in places a haze of pale blue naturalized lupins. Aquilega, broom, globe flower, bistort and delicately perfumed pink and white dog roses add a rich palette of shades to the riverbank scene.

The Dee is the epitome of a Highland river, the sporting playground of eight generations of Royals. The sight of the effervescent waters, amid a vast amphitheatre of snow-capped mountains, bring to mind the nostalgic words of Queen Victoria, who wrote, 'it always gives me a pang to leave the Highlands'.

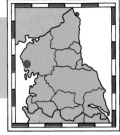
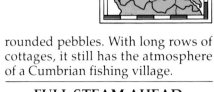

rounded pebbles. With long rows of cottages, it still has the atmosphere of a Cumbrian fishing village.

FULL STEAM AHEAD

Affectionately called 'Little Ratt', the Ravenglass and Eskdale Railway **E** is a 15-inch (38-cm) narrow-gauge steam railway. It was originally built to a 3-feet (91-cm) gauge to carry granite from quarries at the top of Eskdale to the port of Ravenglass, but in 1915 it was modified to the smaller gauge and rebuilt as a

◀ *Muncaster Castle contains many art treasures owned by the Pennington family. 'Little Ratty' (below) transports visitors along Eskdale.*

ALL PHOTOS JOHN WATNEY

FACT FILE

* Ravenglass, off the A595, on the south-west Cumbrian coast

* Outdoor Leisure Map 6, grid reference NY 086964

  miles 0 1 2 3 4 5 6 7 8 9 10 miles
  kms 0 1 2 3 4 5 6 7 8 9 10 11 12 13 14 15 kms

* Allow 2 hours

* Woodland tracks and field paths, some gentle climbs. Stout shoes or boots recommended as there could be mud on forest tracks after rain. Care should be taken on the main road

* **P** Large car park, well signed, in Ravenglass

* **T** British Rail Cumbrian Coast Line between Lancaster, Barrow and Carlisle (except Sundays)

* **WC** Refreshments and toilets at Ravenglass and Eskdale Railway Station. Ratty Arms pub and Pennington Arms Hotel in Ravenglass serve bar meals. Refreshments available at Muncaster Castle (open April-October, closed Mondays)

To a steam railway, a castle known to Shakespeare's Fool and a working watermill

On Lakeland's coast, to the west of the Cumbrian mountains, the village of Ravenglass **A** is situated on an estuary of three small rivers: the Esk, the Mite and the Irt. This easy walk, which begins in the village, takes in a water-powered corn mill, a narrow-gauge steam railway, a Roman bath house and a castle which is still a family home.

The Romans established an important naval base at Ravenglass in the 2nd century, as it was a safe port from which to service the military zone around Hadrian's Wall. The little harbour was also popular with 18th-century smugglers who brought contraband tobacco and French brandy to shore in small boats away from the prying eyes of the excisemen. The main village street leads up from a shingle beach and is paved with smooth sea-

The Roman bath house in Ravenglass, one of many such sites in Cumbria.

tourist line. Having escaped closure in the 1960s, thanks to the efforts of the late Lord Wakefield and an enthusiastic preservation society, it now has 12 superb, small-scale but powerful steam and diesel locomotives. With its trains of open carriages it is one of the most popular and best-loved narrow-gauge railways in the British Isles.

THE WALK

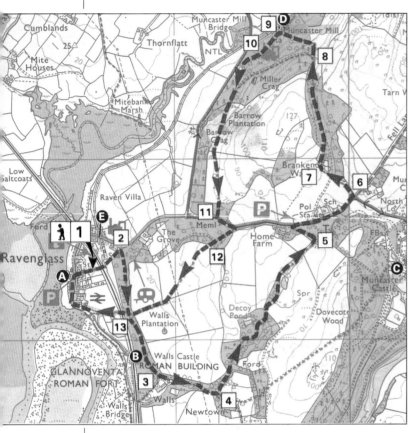

3 At the fork take the track left signposted to Newtown Cottage.

4 Take the next track left, at a footpath sign. This leads past the remains of recently felled woods to a pond (often dry) on the right. Keep ahead through a gate towards the woods.

5 Where the track meets a gate that leads into the grounds of Muncaster Castle **C** do not go through but turn left, following the track as it winds past farm buildings to the main road. Turn right and walk past the Muncaster Castle car park and entrance.

6 Where the main road bends right, go through the gate on the left, along the signposted track towards Brankend Farm.

7 Go through the gate into the farmyard and go right at the bridleway sign. Continue through a wooded valley behind the farm.

8 Where the track bends left, look for a narrower track to the immediate right of a holly tree. It is the middle of a total of three paths forming a three-pronged way, which bears

steeply downhill to Muncaster Mill **D**.

9 Where the tracks cross, turn right to the mill entrance. Return the same way, but do not climb back up the hill left – keep directly ahead on the signposted permissive track back to Ravenglass.

10 Follow this track as it climbs uphill, giving fine coastal views including a glimpse of Sellafield power station. Keep ahead to the main road

11 Turn left on the main road for about 100 yards (80 metres) before crossing to a stile (signposted) on the right and a path that bears diagonally right through the woods.

12 Where the path emerges from the woods, keep in the same direction down a long, sloping field to a gate near the bottom corner of the field ahead. Turn right along the field edge to a gate into the lane.

13 Almost opposite, an enclosed path leads to a tunnel under the railway towards the sea and the end of the village main street for the car park.

RAVENGLASS – MUNCASTER MILL

The walk begins in the public car park at Ravenglass **A**, *alongside Ravenglass Station.*

1 Leave the car park and cross the footbridge over the railway, passing the children's playground with

the terminus of the Ravenglass and Eskdale narrow-gauge railway **E** on the left. Follow the path to its junction with a narrow lane by the main road.

2 Turn right along the lane for about ¹/₂ mile (800 metres), passing the Roman bath house **B**.

Muncaster Mill has been restored to full working order; the grain is stone-ground.

Along the route there is the only surviving part of the Roman fort of Glannoventa. Strategically important to the Romans, it was developed at Ravenglass to protect the harbour. The Roman bath house **B** is a remarkable building and is the tallest surviving free-standing Roman building in Britain, with substantial masonry and well-built walls and doorways, which rise to 12 feet (3.6 metres) in height. It is now in the care of English Heritage and is open to the public.

Less than 1 mile (1.6 km) from Ravenglass is Muncaster Castle **C**. Altered in the 1860s to become a country house, it is set in magnificent gardens, celebrated for superb

rhododendrons and azaleas. Among the paintings in the house is a portrait of Tom Skelton, one of Shakespeare's actors, and a jester, who probably gave his name to 'tomfoolery'.

WATER POWER

Muncaster Mill **D**, on the banks of the River Mite, is a beautifully restored traditional Cumbrian water mill, probably dating from the 18th century, but rebuilt in Victorian times. The machinery can be viewed in action, as can the water courses, millwheel and the drying floor. The mill is open daily, except Saturdays in June to August, from April to October. A variety of wholemeal flours and semolinas are on sale.

FOLLOWING THE RIVER RIBBLE

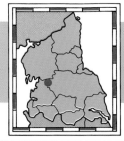

THE NORTH

Through the valley to Stainforth Bridge

Much of this walk is through the gently sloping valley of Upper Ribblesdale, and takes in the beautiful riverside scenery along the Ribble. Trout surface from deep pools in the river bed and at Stainforth Force ➊ the water cascades over limestone steps.

There is an abundance of bird life, including wagtails and busy dippers which dive underwater to search the riverbed for food. Rarer breeds can also be spotted, such as herons and flycatchers. Kestrels hover above their hunting area, and the calls of skylarks, curlews and lapwings fill the air.

TWIN VILLAGES

Stainforth village ➊, with its attractive 17th- and 18th-century stone cottages, is next to Little Stainforth, the twin settlement on the other side of the river. This little hamlet is known for its graceful packhorse bridge ➊ which linked the two villages. It was built by Samuel Watson, a Quaker, in 1675.

The name Stainforth comes from the 'stony ford' which the pack-

▲ *Stainforth Bridge is an ideal spot for picnicking and paddling.*
▶ *Nearby Stainforth Force, where the Ribble tumbles into a pool.*

horse bridge replaced. The river crossing was on a packhorse route between York and Lancaster, which was of major importance during monastic times.

On the fellside above Stainforth, there are medieval cultivation strips ➊ known locally as 'raines'.

Beneath the steep, rocky face of Stainforth Scar ➌, sheep graze the fields. The main breed of the area is Dalesbred, Britain's hardiest breed. They are thought to have been bred by the monks of Fountains Abbey (near Ripon), founded in 1132.

Remains of numerous 19th-century lime-kilns dot the area, and

◀ *Steam trains still run on the popular Settle-Carlisle line, famous for its scenic route. (above) Wild strawberries grow in woods and grassy places.*

FACT FILE

⚹ Stainforth, near Settle, Yorkshire Dales National Park

🗺 Outdoor Leisure Map 10, grid reference SD 820672

miles 0 1 2 3 4 5 6 7 8 9 10 miles
kms 0 1 2 3 4 5 6 7 8 9 10 11 12 13 14 15 kms

🕐 Allow 2 hours

▭ Low-level fields and riverside paths with numerous stiles. Some rough sections and can be muddy in places. Good walking shoes recommended

🅿 In Stainforth, just off B6479

🚆 Settle-Carlisle Railway regular passenger services, also fortnightly/weekly steam trains

🍴 Picnic area signposted from car park. Shop, post office, garage and pub, the Craven Heifer, in Stainforth village

THE WALK

STAINFORTH-LOCKS

The walk begins at the car park in Stainforth **Ⓐ**.

▶**1** Leave the car park and turn left to reach the main road. Keep left for about 500 yards (450 metres) towards Settle.

▶**2** Cross the stone step stile over the dry stone wall. There is a signpost here to Langcliffe. Cross the field in the direction the signpost is pointing, keeping almost parallel to the road. Cross the ladder stile into the next field. These fields lie beneath Stainforth Scar **Ⓒ**. Straight ahead, there is another ladder stile on the far side of the field. Cross this, then after about 60 yards (55 metres), take the steep, stony track past one of the old lime-kilns by Langcliffe Quarry **Ⓓ**. Walk down towards the railway, then across a small field, following a path, to cross a stone stile.

▶**3** Follow the path past the Hoffman kiln **Ⓔ**. Walk through the yard beyond the kiln, and look for a path on the right, opposite a solitary house, next to the railway.

Walk down some steps into a tarmac lane. Turn right, walk under the railway bridge, and cross the main road.

▶**4** Turn left in front of John Roberts' paper recycling mill. Just after the mill, cross the stile on the right where a signpost reads 'FP Locks ½ mile' and go down towards the river. There is a seat on the river bank, conveniently sited for a break. Follow the river bank downstream to the weir at Locks, a hamlet, crossing the dry stone walls by stiles. The last one is a stone step stile.

▶**5** Turn right to cross the river by the footbridge at the weir **Ⓕ**. Take the riverside path on the right. The signpost at the first stile reads 'Footpath to Stainforth Bridge 1.5 m'. From here the path hugs the river bank all the way to Stainforth Bridge, passing beech, lime and sweet chestnut trees **Ⓖ**, and Stainforth Force **Ⓗ**. Cross the bridge **Ⓘ**, and follow the lane uphill to the main road.

▶**6** Turn right for the village and car park.

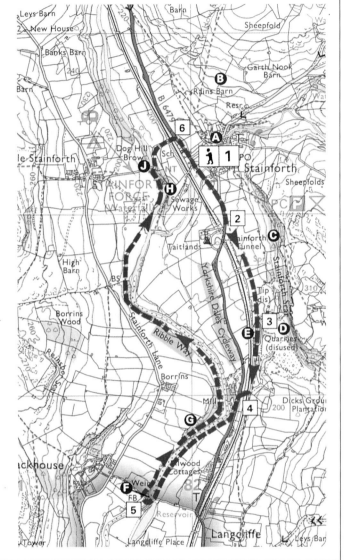

at Langcliffe Quarry **Ⓓ**, there is a well-preserved Hoffman lime-kiln **Ⓔ**. This impressive structure was in use from 1873 to 1939. To produce a constant supply of lime (used to fertilize the moors and improve grazing) there was a series of chambers in the oval-shaped tunnel. The fire progressed slowly around the tunnel, firing each chamber in sequence.

LEAPING SALMON

Another 19th-century industry, cotton spinning, was sited at the weir **Ⓕ**, which was originally constructed to provide a head of water to drive a water mill. Shallow steps have now been built to by-pass the weir, allowing salmon to make their way upstream to breed.

A stretch of attractive woodland **Ⓖ** grows by the Ribble, containing fine specimens of beech, lime and sweet chestnut. Wild flowers surround the Hoffman kiln: yellow ragwort, ox-eye daisy, wild strawberry, clover and bird's foot trefoil can all be seen.

In the 18th and 19th centuries, lime-kilns spring up across the Dales. This Hoffman kiln (left and above), which now stands empty, is unique in Britain.

THE NORTH

SUE MORRIS. INSET: L. CAMPBELL/NHPA

Railways and waterfalls in superb moorland countryside

Goathland, in the North York Moors National Park, is an ancient settlement surrounded by moorland some 500 feet (150m) above sea level. In late summer, the stone buildings bask in a sea of purple heather. From the time of Henry III to the present day, the common land in and around the village has belonged to the Duchy of Lancaster. Today, Goathland is one of Yorkshire's most popular villages. Many of its visitors come to see the steam trains of the North Yorkshire Moors Railway (see box) which stop at the station here.

FRIENDLY SHEEP

The route goes around the edge of the village, but it is worth exploring the centre before you start. The houses straggle along a wide street

FACT FILE

⚹ Goathland, 8 miles (12.8km) south-west of Whitby, off the A169

🗺 Outdoor Leisure Map 27, grid reference NZ 827007

miles 0	1	2	3	4	5	6	7	8	9	10 miles
kms 0	1 2	3	4 5	6	7	8	9 10	11 12	13 14	15 kms

🕒 Allow 3 hours

▬ Steep, rocky and muddy climbs; strenuous in parts. Walking boots are essential. Not suitable for young children

🅿 By the green at the start, or at the car park in the centre of Goathland

🚆 Buses operated by York & City District, Tel. (01653) 692556. The North Yorkshire Moors Railway runs from Grosmont (connecting with BR Whitby) and Pickering April-October, Tel. (01751) 472508

🏨🍴 Mallyan Spout Hotel at the start, and other hotels, pubs and tea-rooms in Goathland; the Birch Hall Inn in Beck Hole

🚻 At car park and Goathland Station

▲*From the path south of Goathland Station, locomotives can be watched climbing through the moors. The tiny harvest mouse (left) lives on the North York Moors, but is not often seen.*

with open grassland on either side. The grass is kept neatly trimmed by black-faced sheep, which wander freely and are quite tame. The bus shelters have been gated to keep the sheep out. The flagged causeways along the wide verges probably date from the mid-17th century.

The starting point is the late-Victorian Church of St Mary Ⓐ, which contains two ancient stone objects of interest: a Saxon or early Norman font and a 12th-century altar slab found in the churchyard.

WATERFALL

From Goathland, the route leads down a steep path to the valley of the West Beck, and Mallyan Spout Ⓑ. This fine waterfall, in a lovely setting of fern-covered rocks, can be quite spectacular after heavy rain. The water tumbles 70 feet (21m).

You continue downstream through woodland. By Incline Cottage Ⓒ, the original course of the Whitby to Pickering Railway can be seen. It is now used as a walking trail. In the early years of the

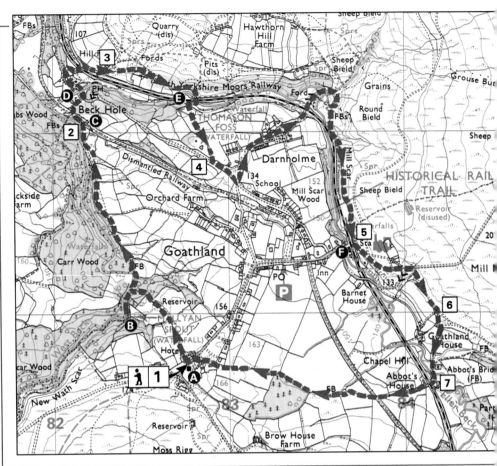

▲ *The enchanting Mallyan Spout, one of the country's best loved waterfalls, plunges over rocks shrouded by ferns.*

railway, carriages were uncoupled at the foot of the 1 in 5 incline, and hauled to the top by a horse-powered rope system. A stationary steam-engine eventually replaced the horses, but this did not prevent Charles Dickens from commenting that he had travelled on a 'quaint old railway along part of which passengers are hauled by a rope'.

RUNAWAY TRAIN

The line was dogged by a number of mishaps, including a derailment when an entire train plunged into a swamp near Goathland. On another occasion, a train laden with herring went out of control, and left a fishy smell hanging over the area for weeks. The Beckhole Incline was closed after a fatal accident in 1864, when the rope snapped and the

▶ *It is hard to imagine that the tranquil hamlet of Beck Hole was once at the centre of a busy iron industry.*

coaches overturned at the bottom, killing two commercial travellers and injuring 13 other people. A safer route between Grosmont and Goathland was opened in 1865.

Beyond the track bed is the hamlet of Beck Hole **D**, one of the gems of Yorkshire. Nestling in a wooded fold of the moors, the cottages cluster round a village green where sheep wander and the locals play

quoits. The focal point of Beck Hole is the Birch Hall Inn, which also serves as the village shop and a café.

It is surprising to discover that, in 1858, two blast furnaces and 33 stone cottages were built here, for no trace of the iron industry or the homes of the 180 workers remains today. Production ceased after only two years, following a series of disastrous incidents, including the

THE WALK

GOATHLAND – DARNHOLME

The walk starts at Goathland's church **Ⓐ**.

1 Cross the road and take the footpath to the right of the hotel, signposted to Mallyan Spout. The path descends steeply to the river. Follow the waymarked footpath left to view the waterfall **Ⓑ**, then retrace your steps and follow the path signposted to Beck Hole. You head uphill, with the river below on your left, and eventually drop steeply again to Incline Cottage **Ⓒ**.

2 Bear left and follow the main track. Go through a gate on your right, then along the lane. Pass through a gate and turn left along the road. Continue through the hamlet of Beck Hole **Ⓓ**. The road curves sharply right and up a steep hill. Just beyond the railway line, take the lane right, to Hill Farm.

3 By the farm, take the main path right (surfaced with chippings). Follow the farm track past a cottage to a natural amphitheatre in the hillside. Keep to the path across the hillside, with the river and Water Ark Foss **Ⓔ** in the trees below on your right. Descend to a footbridge over the river and under the railway. Climb the steps opposite and cross the stile at the top. Turn left along the edge of the field. Climb a stile and follow the narrow lane between hedges to a gate onto a road.

4 Turn left and continue to the crossroads at Darnholme. Turn left through the village and down across the railway. Cross Eller Beck at a ford with stepping stones. Take the path right, along the valley, climbing steeply up steps by the railway line. With the wall on your right, follow the path to Goathland Station **Ⓕ**.

5 Go through the gate to visit the station, then rejoin the path, which climbs along the valley side and curves left by a group of cottages, to a road. Cross, and continue ahead down a tarmac lane almost opposite, until the farm (Goathland House) is directly ahead.

6 Take the signposted footpath diagonally right, downhill, over a waymarked stile and down a narrow valley. At the lower end, cross a footbridge. Go through the gate to the right of the bungalow, and cross another footbridge. Keep right of the farm buildings and go through the gate.

7 Pass under the railway bridge, and continue past Abbot's House up the lane. At the junction with the disused railway, continue ahead into a camping field. With the hedge on your left, continue to the end of the field. Climb a stile and turn right, then climb another stile. Follow the obvious path across fields to emerge on the green by Goathland's church, where the walk began.

---

collapse of one of the furnaces.

The moorland path above Beck Hole follows the Eller Beck Valley, though the river is mostly hidden far below among the trees. At the foot of a natural hillside amphitheatre, up from Thomason Foss, the beck drops over Water Ark Foss **Ⓔ**.

UNDER AND OVER

You will have to scramble down the hillside paths from the main route to view the foss, but the railway, which also winds through the valley, is more easily visible. The path drops to cross the beck by a footbridge under the skew railway bridge, and there is a magnificent view, from the opposite slope, along the line as it curves south towards Darnholme.

The road at Darnholme ends at a shallow ford over the Eller Beck, and the grassy banks by the stepping stones are ideal for a picnic. On a hot day, it is refreshing to paddle in the clear, pebble-strewn stream.

The path continues up a steep slope and along the top of Mill Scar. The railway cutting below was made in 1865 to carry the new line replacing the Beckhole Incline. Its construction was not without problems. Huge boulders had to be blasted away, and rock falls were so frequent that watchmen had to patrol the line every night.

At Goathland Station **Ⓕ**, you can view engines and rolling-stock owned by the North York Moors

▶ *Just upstream from Water Ark Foss, the path leads under a railway bridge and over the lively Eller Beck via a footbridge. From the top of the steps on the far side (far right), engines can be seen shunting their carriages up the hill.*

BOTH PHOTOS: SUE MORRIS

The Grosmont-Pickering Steam Railway

There are few more pleasant ways of viewing this delightful part of the North York Moors National Park than from a train steaming along the 18-mile (28.8-km) line between Grosmont and Pickering.

The line winds through wooded valleys and across open moorland, with stations at Goathland, Newtondale and Levisham. There is a regular steam-hauled service from spring through to the autumn, with special excursions and gala days throughout the year.

The railway's wide-ranging collection of steam and diesel locomotives is continually changing. Favourites include the LMS-built Black Five *George Stephenson*, the massive 2-10-0 *Dame Vera Lynn*, the diminutive colliery workhorse No 5, and a GWR tank engine.

The railway's history stretches back to 1831, when George Stephenson was asked to build a horse tramroad between Whitby and Pickering for transporting coal inland, and limestone, agricultural produce and timber to the coast.

Work proceeded quickly, considering the difficult terrain. A 120-yard (108-m) tunnel had to be constructed at Grosmont. The incline between Beck Hole and Goathland was another major engineering challenge, and special problems were posed by the 20-foot-deep (6-m) Fen Bog at the summit of the incline. The line was formally opened on 26 May 1836, and was an instant success with passenger traffic as well as goods.

The massive costs of construction and operation, however, meant the line was plagued by financial difficulties from the start. It was purchased by the York & North Midland Railway in 1844, and by 1846 there was steam between Pickering and Whitby.

With the increase in private motoring after World War II, and the ravages of the Beeching Plan in the 1960s, the line looked set to close forever. It was saved by the formation of the North York Moors Railway Preservation Society; after years of hard volunteer work, the Grosmont-Pickering stretch was formally re-opened in 1973. Since then, it has proved one of North Yorkshire's most popular attractions.

One of the railway's fiery leviathans pulls into Goathland Station, evoking memories of the golden days of steam.

Historical Railway Trust. If your timing is right, you will see a train steam into the station, and it is fun to stand on the new footbridge wreathed in clouds of steam and smoke. Even when there are no trains there is plenty to see, including the North Eastern signals, a tiny signal box, water cranes and the goods shed, which is used for the restoration of carriages.

The route climbs back onto the open moorland and there are fine views of the railway rising to the south through the heather. Directly ahead on the moors is the alien-looking bulk of the Fylingdales Early Warning Station.

Close to the station stands the Lilla Cross, a Bronze Age monolith that was turned into a Christian cross to commemorate a 7th-century

◀ *This stone 'rimmer' in Goathland was used for forming iron tyres around cart wheels. At Darnholme, the route crosses Eller Beck on stepping stones (below).*

thane, Lilla, who died trying to save the life of King Edwin. The war memorial in Goathland is a replica of the Lilla Cross.

You pass underneath the railway again, and walk past a reminder of Goathland's ancient past; Abbot's House is built on the site of a hermitage mentioned in records from 1100. You cross the disused incline railway again, then return across fields, surrounded by gloriously colourful moorland slopes, to Goathland's church, and the start.

ALL PHOTOS: SUE MORRIS

BY CLIFFTOP AND GOLDEN LINE

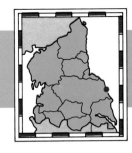

Explore a spectacular coast and the remains of a famous railway

Scalby is an ancient manor on the outskirts of Scarborough. In the 12th and 13th centuries it was part of a royal forest, and it still belongs to the Duchy of Lancaster. An avenue of limes, known locally as 'the Apostles', leads from its High Street to the 12th-century Church of St Laurence **A**. In early summer, pink coral-root bittercress carpets the churchyard. This rare flower is otherwise known only in three or four sites in southern England and one in Staffordshire, so its appearance here is something of a mystery.

The route passes through lanes and fields to the coast, where there is a magnificent view **B** south towards Scarborough's North Bay. The castle on its headland stands nearly 300 feet (90m) above the waves, and the massive Norman keep forms an impressive silhouette.

The route continues north, along the Cleveland Way **C**, a long-distance path that runs beside the coast and around the North York Moors National Park. The walk along the cliffs is exhilarating, and there is much to see. Boats from Scarborough's fishing fleet inspect

▲ *From Hundale Point, as you head north on the Cleveland Way along the coast, there is a splendid view ahead. The butterfish (inset) can be seen in the nearby rock pools. Cloughton Station (below right) was on the Golden Line.*

FACT FILE

- ☀ Scalby, 2 miles (3.2km) north of Scarborough, on the A171

- ▱ Outdoor Leisure Map 27, grid reference TA 010905

  miles 0 1 2 3 4 5 6 7 8 9 10 miles
  0 1 2 3 4 5 6 7 8 9 10 11 12 13 14 15 kms

- ◔ Allow 4 hours

- ▬ Mainly level paths, but a few short, steep ascents and descents. Cliff path muddy and overgrown in stretches, and exposed to wind and sudden mists — wear boots and windproof clothing. The unfenced cliff paths are unsuitable for small children

- P In Scalby's streets

- T BR Scarborough, and a regular bus service from there to Scalby

- ⊠ Pubs and tea-rooms in Scalby

- WC Opposite the post office at the start

their nets, and many pleasure and working boats ply the coast.

The rocky cliffs and beaches are home to many species of gull. Kittiwakes, fulmar, common terns, cormorants, redshanks and oyster-catchers can also be spotted, and, in winter, ringed plovers, turnstones and curlews. Red-throated divers are occasional visitors.

At low tide, there is access down the cliffs to the rocky shore at Crook Ness. Seaweeds and shellfish abound here, and crabs and starfish lurk in the rock pools, where the eel-like butterfish (or gunnel) and the common blenny swim around the fronds of green sea-lettuce. Further along is Cloughton Wyke **D**, favoured by geologists as the rock strata are very clearly visible.

REDUNDANT RAILWAY

You head inland to Cloughton, and join the track of the Scarborough-Whitby railway **E**. This 21-mile (34-km) single-track line opened in 1885 to cater for tourists. Nick-named the Golden Line, it was one of the most scenic routes in Britain, running over 60 bridges, two viaducts and many cuttings and embankments, as well as through two tunnels. Though popular with summer holidaymakers, lack of winter traffic forced it to close in 1965.

Cloughton's station building is now a private house, and you can still see the goods yard, with its cattle dock, and the goods shed. Today, the track bed is a bridlepath, a haven for the wildlife and flowers that line the return walk to Scalby.

THE WALK

SCALBY – CLOUGHTON

The walk starts outside the post office in the High Street of Scalby.

1 With the post office on your right, walk along the High Street, over the junction of North Street and South Street, to the Church of St Laurence **A**. Return along the High Street, and continue past the start to the A171.

2 Cross and continue down Station Road opposite, which eventually becomes Field Lane. At the T-junction, turn right. After just over 100 yards (90m), turn left over a stile. Follow the signposted field-edge path ahead to the clifftop, from which there is a fine view **B**.

3 Turn left and follow the waymarked Cleveland Way **C** along the coast to where the path goes inland at Cloughton Wyke **D**. Return to the coast, climb a stile and follow the path for about 50 paces. Turn left into a small car park and continue inland along the tarmac lane (Salt Pans Road) to the junction with the A171 at Cloughton.

4 Cross and bear right along the A171. Just before Little Moor Close, turn left over a stone stile. Follow the signposted path between gardens and along the left edge of a cricket field. Continue alongside Cloughton Beck, crossing the road at a ford. At the end of a large, grassy field, the path bends sharp left. Go through a metal gate and walk along a lane, with a cemetery on your right, to a road.

5 Cross, and walk down Station Lane opposite. At the end of the houses, turn

right on a path in front of the old station buildings, through the picnic area and onto the old railway **E**. Follow this to where it meets the A165.

6 Cross, and rejoin the old track via a wooden gate just beyond Hawthorn Close. Walk along Lancaster Way. Turn left into Field Close Road, then turn right into Station Road. Retrace your steps from here to the start.

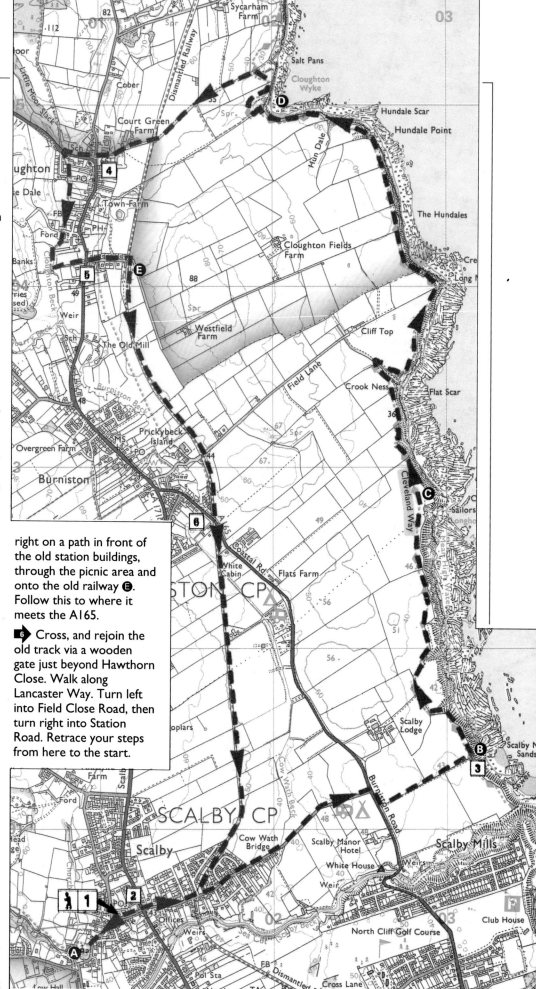

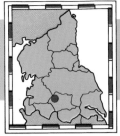

THE BRONTE MOORS

A beautiful walk around the country that inspired *Wuthering Heights*

This walk explores some of the most evocative landscape of the Yorkshire Pennines. The desolate moors, which so inspired the Brontë sisters, rise majestically above the steep-sided valleys — a vast expanse of treeless moorland, crag and heather through which narrow streams and cloughs (gorges) twist their way, forming little valleys of delicate beauty.

Drystone walls criss-cross the hillsides in elaborate patterns, punctuated by barns and remote farmhouses, many of them dating from the 17th century, and some clustered in hamlets and villages that have changed little over the centuries. This upland landscape contrasts, often starkly, with the bustling Victorian mill towns and

FACT FILE

- Haworth, West Yorkshire

- Pathfinder 682 (SE 03/13) and Outdoor Leisure Map 21, grid reference SE 029372

| miles 0 | 1 | 2 | 3 | 4 | 5 | 6 | 7 | 8 | 9 | 10 miles |
| kms 0 | 1 2 3 | 4 5 6 | 7 8 | 9 10 11 | 12 13 | 14 | 15 kms |

- 5 hours

- Paths can be muddy and overgrown. Sturdy footwear (preferably walking boots) strongly recommended

- **P** Haworth Parsonage car park, at top of village. There are alternative car parks in the village at busy times

- **T** Park-and-ride steam train service from Keighley, or Ingrow to Haworth Station at weekends and holiday times, avoid congestion

- **WC** In Haworth and Oakworth

- Wide choice of refreshments in Haworth. Pubs in Stanbury and Oakworth

industry in the larger valleys, including Haworth itself, still served by a restored steam railway.

The old part of Haworth Ⓐ has a steep, cobbled Main Street, leading down from the church, with alleys and courts branching off it, but the village expanded in Victorian times, stretching down the hillside towards the river and railway.

DARK SATANIC MILLS

At the time of the Brontës this was a thriving and squalid early industrial town. It was towns like Haworth that provided the backbone of Victorian industrial wealth. Many of the older cottages still retain their weaving lofts, with their multipaned windows to provide the weavers with maximum light. These lofts pre-dated the new water and steam-powered mills.

Haworth had grown rapidly at the beginning of the 19th century and was overcrowded and without any sanitation or proper drainage.

▲ *The wild bleakness of Haworth Moor and the ruins of Top Withens were the inspiration for* **Wuthering Heights.** *(inset) Wild moorland harebells.*
▼ *The steep Main Street of Haworth.*

THE WALK

HAWORTH – STANBURY – OAKWORTH

The walk begins at the Brontë Parsonage Museum in Haworth Ⓐ.

1 Walk down the hill towards the church Ⓑ; turn right through a kissing gate below the churchyard, along an enclosed stone-paved way.

2 At the footpath junction turn right, signposted Brontë Falls, up to the road. Sowden's Farm Ⓓ is across fields on the left. Cross the road and enter the Penistone Hill Country Park. Take the narrow footpath bearing left across the moor ahead and Penistone Hill Ⓔ. Continue over the brow of the hill.

3 Keep left around the edge of the old quarry and follow the clear track round to the right, before eventually bearing left down to the road.

4 Walk a few yards down the road and then take the track on the right to Drop Farm. Continue straight ahead with the wall on your left to a footpath junction. Follow the line of yellow posts across the moorland.

5 At the track turn left. Just before the farm take the footpath on the right, cross

over the bridge and walk down a shallow ravine to Brontë Falls Ⓕ.

6 Cross the stream at the stone bridge — Brontë Bridge — and head directly up the hill. Go through the gate and turn right towards Stanbury. Follow the footpath to a track and turn right into the village of Stanbury Ⓖ.

7 Walk to the far end of the village and take the green lane on the left that runs behind the village. Continue for about 150 yards (135 metres) and then go through a gate on the right, following a field path down to a stream. Cross the

The Parsonage at Haworth was home to the remarkable Brontë family and now houses Brontë memorabilia.

Also, refuse was simply left to rot in the streets. Not surprisingly, disease, particularly typhoid, was rife. Even in the 1850s half the children died before they were six and the average life expectancy was 25 years old — figures that equalled the worst London slums.

This high mortality rate led to overcrowding in the graveyard, until finally the old Parish Church,

with its cottage windows, had to be pulled down in 1879 because of the excessive number of bodies in its vaults and in the nearby graveyard. It was threatening the very health of the town. And it is quite sobering to realize that the Parsonage obtained all its drinking water from a well sunk into the ground of that cemetery. The present church Ⓑ, built in 1880, has a chapel in memory of the Brontë family.

Behind the church is the Black Bull Inn Ⓒ where Branwell Brontë spent much of his time. He drank

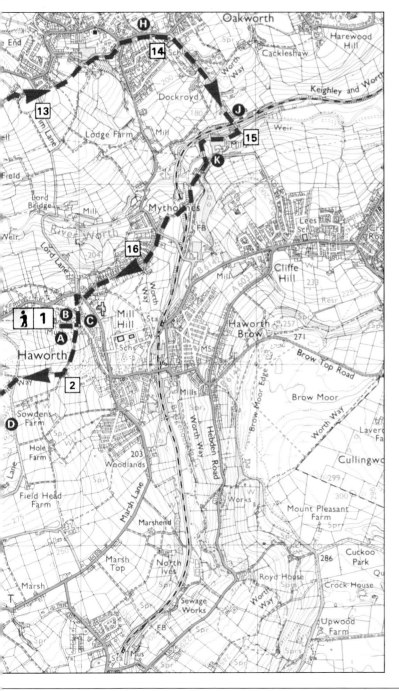

bridge and continue uphill to another gate, pass through a third gate and go up the field to a farm track. Turn right on to the path leading to Manor House Farm at Oldfield.

▪8▶ Continue straight ahead through two small gates, through a farm, following a field path to West House Farm. Look for a small stile in the wall. Cross the stile to pass the farm house on the left. Bear right and then go straight ahead to a small gap in the wall. Follow the field path until arriving at a track.

▪9▶ Continue straight ahead with a barn on the right, through a gate to a second track. Walk up the embankment to go through a gap in the wall opposite and follow the field path past a new house to take the gate on the left to the road.

▪10▶ Turn right and as the road bends and goes uphill, walk through the small gap in the wall on the right and follow the field path to a farm. Go through a gate, turn right and cross the farmyard to another gate opposite a barn.

▪11▶ Cross two fields and continue straight ahead along a walled track between a row of cottages. As the track bends to the right cross the stone stile to the left of the house. Follow the stone stiles across the fields until reaching a farm track.

▪12▶ Turn left up the hill to a stile and continue across fields to a farm. Turn left, following the track right round the farm to a gate. Follow the field path to another farm and then turn right down a track to the road.

▪13▶ Cross the road and go over a small stone stile on the right. Continue along the footpath, crossing a track down to an old mill. Here, the path may become overgrown with nettles during the summer. Turn right and continue to road junction. Follow the Colne Road downhill past Holden Park **H** .

▪14▶ Continue to the bottom of the hill. Turn right down Station Road to arrive at Oakworth Railway Station **J** .

▪15▶ Walk along the road past Vale Mill **K** and over the bridge. Reach Valefold Cottages and take the footpath to Mytholmes Lane.

▪16▶ At the road continue uphill into Haworth and to the Parsonage at the start of the walk.

himself to an early grave with a mixture of Yorkshire ale and opium.

FIRE AND BRIMSTONE

Just outside Haworth is a 17th-century farmhouse **D** that became the setting for 18th-century revivalist meetings led by the English Evangelical preacher William Grimshaw. Grimshaw was a close friend of John Wesley and his fiery zeal attracted congregations from miles around, with meetings often continuing until five o'clock in the morning. Grimshaw would often leave during the Psalm to bring in idlers off the street and from public houses to hear his sermon.

Penistone Hill **E** appears in *Wuthering Heights* as Penistone Crags, a local beauty spot near Thrushcross Grange. The quarry here provided the stone for the paving blocks in the high street, and for the dark buildings of Haworth. Looking at the now disused gritstone quarries on the edge

'Owd Timmy', the last handloom weaver, enjoying a pipe at his cottage.

BRADFORD ART GALLERIES AND MUSEUMS

of the moor it is hard to imagine that as late as the 1920s a hundred men hewed stone here. Penistone Hill is now a 180 acre (73 hectare) Country Park and from the summit there is a spectacular view across the bleak, open Pennines.

WUTHERING HEIGHTS

Brontë Falls **F**, which tumble into Salden Beck, was a favourite spot with the Brontë sisters and is described in their poems and letters. A few yards down the stream is the Brontë seat which is hewn out of a single piece of rock. And high up on the Moors is Top Withens, the ruin of a lonely farmhouse which is said to have been the inspiration for Emily Brontë's well-loved novel *Wuthering Heights*.

The Brontë Falls (top) were a favourite haunt of the sisters and much of their poetry is deeply descriptive of the moods of the countryside surrounding Haworth. The Brontë seat (above) may well have witnessed the first few words of a novel.

Stanbury **G** is a typical Pennine moorland village. It was the home of Timothy Feather, known as 'Owd Timmy', the last handloom weaver in Yorkshire. The steam-powered West Riding mills of the 19th century saw the demise of this old cottage industry, but 'Owd Timmy' pursued his craft until his death in 1910 aged 85. His loom is on display in Cliffe Castle Museum in nearby Keighley.

Holden Park **H** was once the home of Sir Isaac Holden, but is now a delightful and unusual garden laid out in his memory by his grandson, Francis Illingworth. Surrounding the bowling green are elaborate stone grottos and walkways that are a delight to explore.

THE DAYS OF STEAM

Oakworth Station **J**, which is on the Keighley and Worth Valley line has been beautifully restored as a Victorian country halt, albeit with a 1950s flavour. Old advertisements, a genteel ladies' waiting room, a ticket machine and gaslights all add to the atmosphere. On the platform stand milk churns and old-fashioned leather luggage still waiting to be collected, and the staff are dressed in immaculate period costume. This was the station used for the film *The Railway Children*.

The 4½ mile (7.2 km) Keighley and Worth Valley Railway is one of the finest restored steam railways in the country and runs regular daily steam services in the summer, and

at weekends during the winter months. The railway was originally opened in 1867, not only to carry passengers but also to bring raw materials to the valley's mills, like Vale Mill which lies close to Oakworth Station.

Vale Mill **K** dates from the 1780s and, as in many other Yorkshire mills, cotton was originally spun here. During the 19th century the mill eventually turned to worsted manufacturing and developed into the present elaborate complex.

Vale Mill was once owned by a strict Methodist family, the Sugdens, and the employees were forbidden to drink or to gamble, and those courting couples that 'got into trouble' either had to marry or face losing their jobs.

The walk can be shortened by catching a train at Oakworth Station back to Haworth.

The beautifully restored station at Oakworth is a perfect period piece.

The Four Brontës

Charlotte, Emily, Anne and their brother Branwell developed an intense creative partnership which was to lead to the writing of some of the greatest novels of 19th-century English fiction, including Charlotte's *Jane Eyre* and *Villette*, Emily's *Wuthering Heights* and Anne's *Tenant of Wildfell Hall*. Only Branwell failed to fulfil his early promise and died of a broken heart, opium and drink.

THURSTASTON HILL

A gentle walk to superb views of the surrounding countryside

Thurstaston Hill overlooks the magnificent Dee Estuary, a 30,000 acre (90 hectare) expanse of mudflats and salt marsh and a vital feeding ground for migrating birds. Thurstaston Hill itself, a heathland covered in gorse, heather and birch, is only 298 feet (90 metres) high, but it provides some of the most spectacular views in the Wirral.

COUNTRY PARK

Wirral Country Park was one of the first country parks to be established under the 1968 Countryside Act and follows the line of the old Hooton-West Kirby railway. Details of the area are provided at the Thurstaston Visitor Centre **Ⓐ**. Running through the park is the 12-mile (19-km) Wirral Way **Ⓑ**, which for over half of its length runs directly parallel to the Dee Estuary.

The first section of the Hooton to Parkgate railway was opened in 1866 and it was later extended to West Kirby in 1868. The line was

SEFTON PHOTO LIBRARY. INSET: J. F. REYNOLDS/NATURE PHOTOGRAPHERS LTD

▲ *The mudflats of the Dee Estuary make a perfect stopping-off place for migrating birds. The knot (inset) visits in autumn and spring on its way between Africa and the Arctic.*

originally built to serve the Neston colliery and there were plans to extend the line over the Dee Estuary to Flint on the Welsh coast. It was closed in 1956 and the track bed removed in 1962. Today the old line forms the backbone of the country park, but you can still see the old station platforms, bridges, railway cuttings and embankments.

At various places along the Wirral Way there are viewing points across the Dee Estuary **Ⓒ**. At low tide you can see the great expanse of

mud and sandbanks, which in late summer and autumn become the home of great flocks of migrating birds including oyster catchers, shelducks, Canada geese and cormorants. During the winter months it is also an important wintering ground for waders and ducks.

VIEW OF WALES

Caldy Hill **Ⓓ**, a delightful sandstone ridge shaded by Scots pines, affords superb views over the estuary to Anglesey and on towards the Great Orme headland at Llandudno. On the summit of Thurstaston Hill stands a stone viewpoint **Ⓔ** depicting a map of the surrounding coastline. From here across the estuary are Wales, the Clwydian

FACT FILE

✳	Thurstaston Country Park, Wirral
▱	Pathfinder 738 (SJ 28/38), grid reference SJ 238834

miles 0 1 2 3 4 5 6 7 8 9 10 miles
kms 0 1 2 3 4 5 6 7 8 9 10 11 12 13 14 15 kms

◔	3 hours
▭	Easy walking along a disused railway and heathland paths
P	Thurstaston Visitor Centre
T	Trains to West Kirby to join the walk 1 mile (1.6 km) along the Wirral Way at Stage 2
WC	
▤	The Cottage Loaf pub at Thurstaston
♍	Thurstaston Visitor Centre

THE WALK

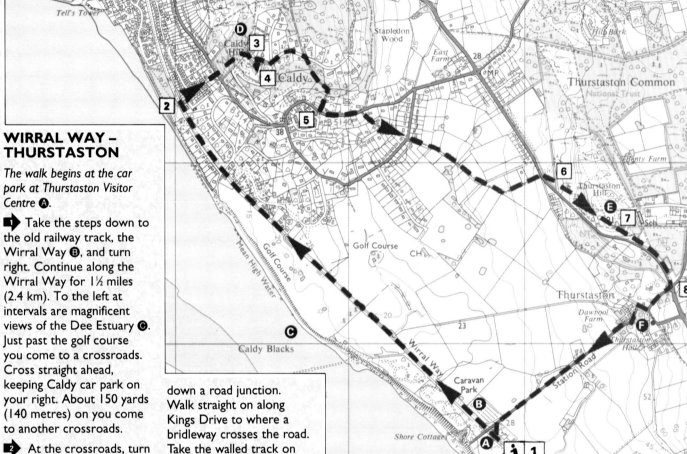

WIRRAL WAY – THURSTASTON

The walk begins at the car park at Thurstaston Visitor Centre **Ⓐ**.

1 Take the steps down to the old railway track, the Wirral Way **Ⓑ**, and turn right. Continue along the Wirral Way for 1½ miles (2.4 km). To the left at intervals are magnificent views of the Dee Estuary **Ⓒ**. Just past the golf course you come to a crossroads. Cross straight ahead, keeping Caldy car park on your right. About 150 yards (140 metres) on you come to another crossroads.

2 At the crossroads, turn right to a gate and continue up the road towards Caldy Hill **Ⓓ**. At the road junction, cross over to the gap in the fence almost directly opposite. Follow the small path up the hill towards a stony knoll and bench. Bear right to a gap in the stone wall.

3 Take the path on the left signed 'West Kirby', up the hill to a rocky pine-covered ridge.

4 Keep right and drop

down a road junction. Walk straight on along Kings Drive to where a bridleway crosses the road. Take the walled track on the right and at the road bear right. Take the path on the right marked by a white metal sign to Thurstaston.

5 At the B5140 turn left, crossing the road at the T-junction to follow the waymarked track ahead. At the next road take the footpath opposite, to Thurstaston Common.

6 Follow the footpath through the heathland, keeping left and following the faint path ascending

gently between two rocky outcrops. Take the path on the left up to the ridge. At the ridge turn right to the viewpoint **Ⓔ**.

7 From the viewpoint walk to the white cairn and then take the path on the right. Ignore the first turning on the right, but take the second, which drops down to a car park. Turn left and go through a

gap in the fence signed picnic site, following a path that leads to a wooden stile and the road.

8 Turn right along the road past the Cottage Loaf Pub. At the crossroads turn right along Station Road to Thurstaston village **Ⓕ**. At the village continue down Station Road to Thurstaston country park and the start of the walk.

Hills and Snowdonia's Carnedd Llwelyn, while across the Wirral Plain lies Liverpool. Further north, on a clear day it is sometimes possible to see Blackpool Tower and Black Combe in the Lake District.

Thurstaston village **Ⓕ**, built

◀*The view from the top of Caldy Hill over the Dee Estuary to Clywd and the Welsh hills.*

around a green, is now a conservation area. The records of the church go back to 1125 but the present red sandstone church is Victorian, built in splendid Gothic style in 1886. A plain stone tower of an early building still stands in the churchyard. Next to the church stands Thurstaston Hall. It is haunted by an old lady, a member of the Glegg family who once owned the Hall.

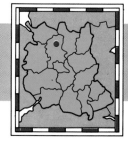

▲*An overgrown limekiln beside Caldon Canal is a reminder of the valley's industrial past, when the canal (below) was an important transport route. It has now been restored for leisure use. The cardinal beetle (left) can be seen on flowers in May and June.*

the old village lies up an old sunken lane, Hollow Lane, where this walk starts. Folds and terraces of tiny cottages and larger yeomen's houses huddle opposite a 12th-century church of mellow sandstone.

The village's former industrial centre lies below, at the foot of a

FACT FILE

☀ Cheddleton, 3 miles (4.8km) south of Leek, on the A520

🗺 Pathfinders 792 (SJ 85/95), 809 (SJ 84/94) and 810 (SK 04/14), grid reference SJ 971523

miles 0	1	2	3	4	5	6	7	8	9	10 miles
kms 0	1 2 3	4 5	6 7	8 9 10	11 12	13 14 15 kms				

🕐 Allow 5 hours

▬ The route is impassable when the river floods. The river and canal section can be muddy. Several fairly short, steep ascents and descents. Walking boots are recommended

P Car park between the church and the Black Lion pub, on Hollow Lane at the start

T Regular bus service between Leek and Hanley stops in Cheddleton, Tel. (01785) 223344 for details

🍺 Pubs at Cheddleton, Consallforge and Basford Bridge

Follow a little-known river valley to a woodland nature reserve

The north-east corner of Staffordshire gloriously lays the lie that the county has been ruined by heavy industry and potteries. The River Churnet, one of the English countryside's great secrets, winds through a wooded gorge. The scenery is not disturbed by any roads. There was once industry in this valley, but it was served by canal, river, railway and tramways, all of which feature in this peaceful walk.

Cheddleton village ❶ sits astride the ancient trade route between Buxton and Stafford. The heart of

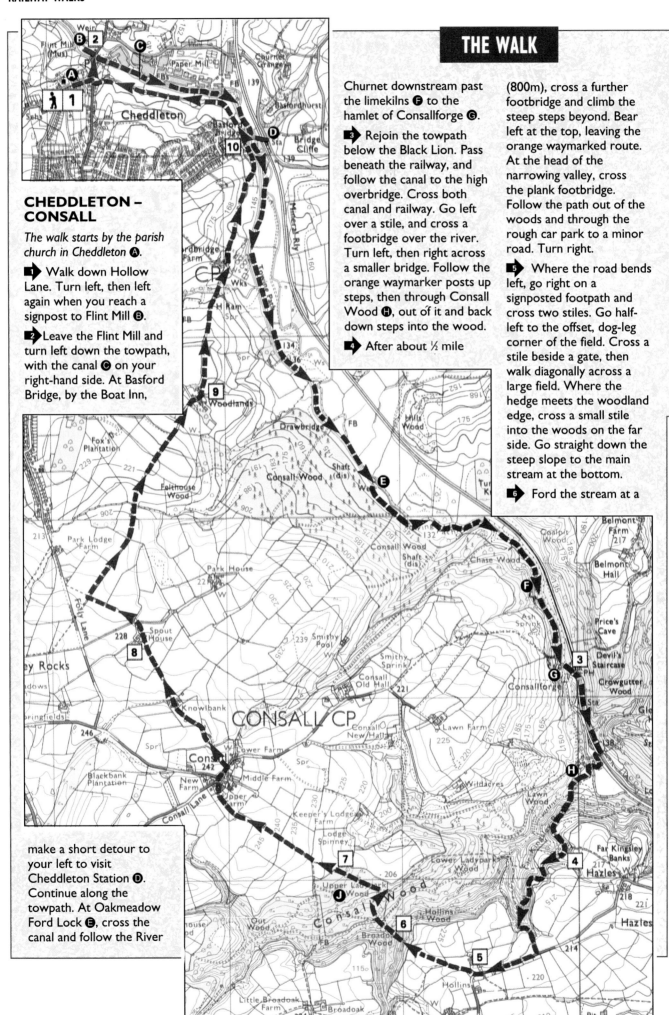

THE WALK

CHEDDLETON – CONSALL

The walk starts by the parish church in Cheddleton ⒶA.

1 Walk down Hollow Lane. Turn left, then left again when you reach a signpost to Flint Mill ⒷB.

2 Leave the Flint Mill and turn left down the towpath, with the canal ⒸC on your right-hand side. At Basford Bridge, by the Boat Inn, make a short detour to your left to visit Cheddleton Station ⒹD. Continue along the towpath. At Oakmeadow Ford Lock ⒺE, cross the canal and follow the River

Churnet downstream past the limekilns ⒻF to the hamlet of Consallforge ⒼG.

3 Rejoin the towpath below the Black Lion. Pass beneath the railway, and follow the canal to the high overbridge. Cross both canal and railway. Go left over a stile, and cross a footbridge over the river. Turn left, then right across a smaller bridge. Follow the orange waymarker posts up steps, then through Consall Wood ⒽH, out of it and back down steps into the wood.

4 After about ½ mile

(800m), cross a further footbridge and climb the steep steps beyond. Bear left at the top, leaving the orange waymarked route. At the head of the narrowing valley, cross the plank footbridge. Follow the path out of the woods and through the rough car park to a minor road. Turn right.

5 Where the road bends left, go right on a signposted footpath and cross two stiles. Go half-left to the offset, dog-leg corner of the field. Cross a stile beside a gate, then walk diagonally across a large field. Where the hedge meets the woodland edge, cross a small stile into the woods on the far side. Go straight down the steep slope to the main stream at the bottom.

6 Ford the stream at a

sharp bend. Just beyond are a capped old shaft and a Nature Reserve sign for Upper Ladypark Wood **J**. Follow the yellow waymark arrows up to and across a wider track. The path is very indistinct. If you lose sight of the waymarks on the trees, or are in any doubt, keep right until you emerge on a wider track beside a pond filled with wiry, dead tree stumps. Go left, then bear right after a few paces along a narrow, waymarked path through the woods, again heading right if in any doubt.

7 Climb a stile out of the woods. Go slightly left to a stile in the far corner.

Follow the hedge to your right, then a field-side farm track to Upper Farm, Consall. Go through the farmyard to a road. Turn right, then left after 100 yards (90m) on the footpath signposted 'Folley Lane'. Cross the stile ahead and go up a long, thin field to Knowlbank Farm. Pass between the farmhouse and a corrugated-iron barn. Cross the farm track and head for Spout House Farm ahead.

8 Walk immediately left of a long barn. Go through the enclosed farmyard and along a drive for 50 yards (45m). At a crossing drive, go through the left-hand gate and follow the line of the rough hedge/fence on your right to a stile. Climb this and turn right. Cross a line of stiles ahead; the path eventually merges with the walled roadway leading to the entrance to Woodlands Hall.

9 Go straight ahead through the overgrown yard into a field beyond. Stay close to a holly hedge on your left. After 100 yards (90m), cross the double stile and continue down the field with the hedge to your left. Keep ahead over another double stile. Climb the next stile and follow the farm track as it winds down through a

ford and up again between a farm and the sewage works. As the concreted road bends right, go through the middle gate ahead and follow a thorn hedge. Go through a gate, and follow the obvious path to the Boat Inn at Basford Bridge.

10 Walk in front of the terrace opposite the pub, and then along the path beyond. Take the second right fork to the canal bank, below some gardens. Remain with this path as it leaves the canal, and walk through a series of fields to return to Cheddleton at the Red Lion Inn, opposite Hollow Lane.

There are working steam locomotives and a museum at Victorian Cheddleton Station. Past Oakmeadow Ford Lock (below left) the canal joins the Churnet.

steep sandstone bluff. Between the river and the canal are an old brewery, warehouses and the marvellous Flint Mill **B** (see box).

For nearly 4 miles (6.4km), the walk follows the Caldon Canal **C**. This was surveyed by the renowned canal-builder James Brindley, though he died before it opened in 1777. It was constructed to convey limestone from the massive quarries at Cauldon to the main Trent and Mersey Canal in Stoke-on-Trent.

RESTORED CANAL

Other uses were soon found for it, associated with the pottery industry, and it was extended to Uttoxeter in 1811. A victim of road and rail competition, it was abandoned in 1944, but in 1974 became the first canal to be fully rescued and restored by enthusiasts and volunteers.

At Basford Bridge, a short detour from the towpath leads to Cheddleton Station **D**. The North Staffordshire Railway Society, based here, plan to operate steam trains between Cheddleton and Froghall. Currently, these fiery leviathans are confined to a short section of track at

▲*The wooded Churnet Valley is a peaceful, unspoiled area today.*

the station. The neo-Gothic building is attributed to the Victorian architect Pugin, best known for his work on the Houses of Parliament.

The walk now follows the wide, flat valley of the Churnet to Oakmeadow Ford Lock **E**, where canal and river join forces at the start of a long, winding gorge.

A little way downstream, the remains of two limekilns **F** are all but hidden in the encroaching woods. Here, limestone from

ALL PHOTOS: JASON SMALLEY

The Flint Mill

There has been a mill at the point of the Churnet where South Mill now stands since the 13th century. Originally a corn mill, then a fulling mill, it was converted to grind flint in around 1800. Another mill, North Mill, had been built beside the same mill stream 40 years earlier for the same purpose. Both survive miraculously intact, their twin undershot wheels working a panoply of machinery dedicated to producing raw materials for the potters in nearby Stoke-on-Trent.

Flint is an important ingredient in the manufacture of fine china and porcelain, to which it gives both strength and whiteness. It is found predominantly in the chalk hills and downs of south-east England; a long journey by coaster and then by

The Flint Mill, which is still powered by water, can be seen in operation, crushing flint for the potteries at Stoke-on-Trent, on Saturday and Sunday afternoons.

narrowboat brought the flint to the canalside at Cheddleton.

There, it was first roasted, then crushed, before being mixed with water and ground to fine powder in the mills. The resultant, soup-like 'slop' was allowed to settle before being dried in a slip kiln, formed into blocks and sent by narrowboat to the potteries. All this occurred on this very compact site, interconnected by

a plateway and a series of pumps worked by the waterwheels.

Dedicated volunteers ensure that the mills are fully operational. South Mill also houses machinery for the crushing of various metallic ores, which give the potter a vast choice of colour to decorate their wares with before glazing. The old miller's cottage adjoining South Mill houses artefacts from centuries past.

ALL PHOTOS: JASON SMALLEY

▲ *Winding between wooded hills and farmland, the Churnet is a place to spot the common sandpiper, a small wader.*

Cauldon was roasted to rid it of impurities, before being transported on a horse-drawn tramway to Weston Coyney, about 7 miles (11.2km) away, and sold for fertilizer, whitewash and many other uses. The grassy track bed of the tramway can be seen disappearing up a wooded side valley above the kilns.

Two signposts, one metal, one sandstone, record the respective canal mileages to Uttoxeter and

Froghall. Etruria, also mentioned on the mileposts, is the junction of the Caldon with the Trent and Mersey.

FIERY FURNACES

Peaceful Consallforge ❻ was once one of the main industrial centres of the upper Churnet. Iron ore and limestone were combined in furnaces to produce pig iron. This was transferred by canal, rail or packhorse to Leek and other locations to be transformed into firegrates, domestic utensils and tinplate.

A great bank of kilns still stands beside the canal, while in Crowgutter Wood, south-east of the hamlet, there are tumbled, ivy-covered walls lost in the woodland. Until very recently, it was all but impossible to reach this spot by car, and most people still arrive by foot or boat, aiming for the characterful Black Lion Inn, which overlooks the lock where river and canal once again separate.

The walk leaves the towpath and enters Consall Wood ❼, an open-access nature reserve managed by the County Council and crisscrossed by waymarked trails. The reserve protects the habitat of dozens of species of birds. The steep, wooded valleys are thick with

▶ *As you near Cheddleton, there are sweeping views over the countryside.*

birch and ash woodland. Beneath the trees are small bricked- or fenced-off shafts, the remains of small-scale coalmining activity that occurred here sporadically over many centuries.

Despite the waymarks, many of the paths are little used and hard to distinguish. This is true, in particular, of those in Upper Ladypark Wood ❽. Between the woods and Consall village, there are extensive views across the rolling countryside to the distinctive range of The Roaches, north of Leek, and the conical shape of Shutlingsloe, south-east of Macclesfield.

Beyond Consall, the route follows field paths through farmland, then follows the opposite bank of the canal to that on the outward route, to return to Cheddleton.

LOOKING HIGH AND LOW

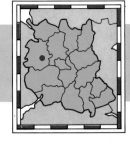

ROBERT EAMES. INSET: ANDREW CLEAVE/NATURE PHOTOGRAPHERS

FACT FILE

✳ Bridgnorth, 13 miles (20.8km) south of Telford, on the A442

🆗 Pathfinder 911 (SO 69/79), grid reference SO 714935

miles 0 1 2 3 4 5 6 7 8 9 10 miles
kms 0 1 2 3 4 5 6 7 8 9 10 11 12 13 14 15 kms

🕐 Allow 3½ hours

▬ Several short ascents and descents. Can be muddy, especially by the river

P Innage Lane car park, off the B4373 north of High Town

T Severn Valley Line from Kidder-minster BR station. Summer, daily; winter, weekends only, Tel. (01299) 403816 for times. Regular buses from all large nearby towns

🍴 Pubs and cafés in Bridgnorth; The Crown Inn at Eardington

WC In the car park at the start and at the station

🏰 Daniel's Mill is open April-September on Wednesdays and weekends, Tel. (01746) 762753 for times

▲From High Town there are views across the River Severn, which is spanned here by a stone bridge, to Low Town. Wallflowers (inset) from local gardens can be found growing wild. The Northgate (below) is Bridgnorth's only surviving medieval gate.

ROBERT EAMES

Around a historic Severnside town on two levels

The town of Bridgnorth has a split personality: Low Town, on the Severn, was a busy river port for centuries, while High Town grew up around the superb strategic position afforded by a sandstone bluff that towers 100 feet (30m) above the river. The two are joined by ancient steps and narrow streets that tumble down the hillside, as well as by Britain's only inland cliff railway. Both have handsome half-timbered

THE WALK

BRIDGNORTH – EARDINGTON

The walk starts from the Innage Lane car park in Bridgnorth.

1 Take the footpath signposted to the town centre. Go through Northgate **A**, then turn left into Church Street to St Leonard's **B**.

2 Descend Granary Steps to Friar Street, and turn right to the junction with Cartway **C**. Bear right up to High Town. At the top, turn left onto Castle Terrace. Either turn down Stoneway Steps to the left or go along Castle Walk to catch the cliff railway **D**. At the bottom, turn right along Underhill Street to Lavington's Hole **E** in the sandstone cliff. Retrace your steps towards the bridge to gain access to the riverside path. Turn right. Follow the river through fields, under the bypass and into woodland. Look out for a pair of gates onto the road on your right.

3 Go through the gates, to Daniel's Mill **F**, then retrace your steps to the river. Turn right and continue along the path, through a long riverside field. When the river bends away from the steep, wooded bank on your right, keep straight ahead, alongside the bank to a stile by two galvanized gates. Continue on this track, curving up a shallow valley to a gate, which leads into Slade Lane. Where the lane bears left near a white cottage, turn right alongside a plantation and cross the railway line by the cottage.

4 Go ahead along a lane to a minor road. Turn right, then soon left up a minor road marked as a cul-de-sac. Continue up this lane, which becomes a rough track and then a grassy byway, for about ½ mile (800m), passing High Downs Farm. After the lane bears sharply to the left, cross the stile on your right into a field. Follow the edge of the woodland on your left. When this ends, bear slightly right, aiming to the right of a brick house, to a stile. Cross, and follow the field edge on your right. Cross another stile, and continue along an overgrown path into the garden of a white cottage. Continue ahead over three more stiles to a road.

5 Turn right, and fairly soon go through a gap in the fence on your left. Head diagonally right across the field to the lowest corner, dropping down some brick steps to cross Potseething Spring. Continue ahead through three more fields, crossing the last one by following a

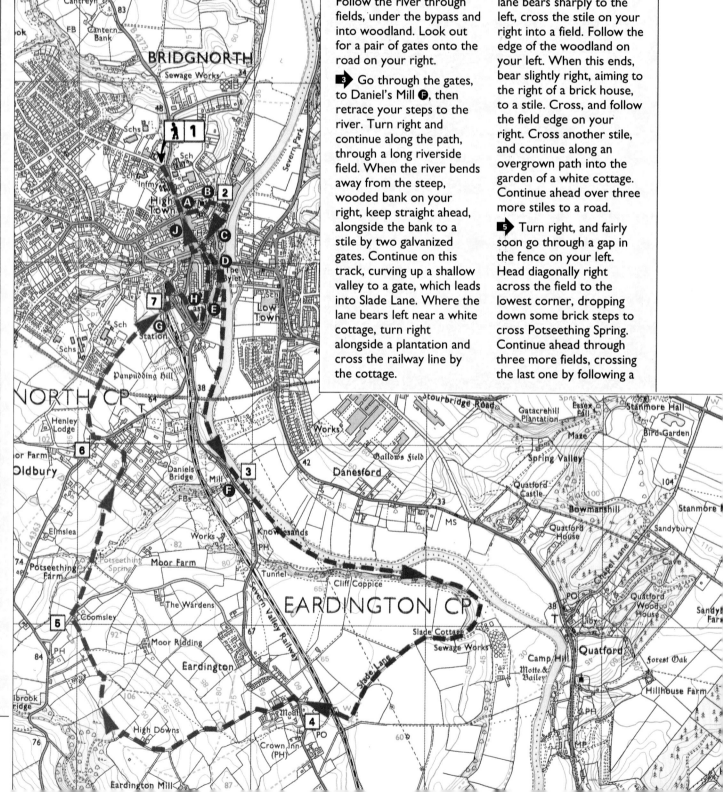

buildings from the 17th century.

This walk enters the old town via Northgate **Ⓐ**, the only survivor of five medieval stone gates. It has undergone extensive rebuilding work, and now houses a museum in the room over its arches.

St Leonard's Church **Ⓑ** occupies the town's highest point. The present building is Victorian, but there has been a church here since the 13th century, and the churchyard is well worth a visit. The area round about is full of interest. On your immediate left is a small half-timbered house where Richard Baxter, the famous Puritan preacher, lived when he was a curate at old St Leonard's, in 1640-41.

Further on, you pass the old grammar school, built in 1629, and

▲*Lavington's Hole was dug in order to blow up the Royalists' munitions.*

three brick-faced, 17th-century houses, formerly a schoolhouse and the homes of the schoolmaster and the vicar. Beyond these are Granary Steps, which lead down to the site of a 13th-century Franciscan friary.

CAVE DWELLERS

Walking along Friar Street, you come to Cartway **Ⓒ**. This was the only route accessible to wheeled vehicles from the river wharves of Low Town up to High Town. The ribbed brick pavements helped prevent pack donkeys from slipping as they climbed. In the sandstone cliff faces are caves, which were inhabited up until 1856. Residents bricked up some of the entrances

and installed proper doors and windows to make life more comfortable.

The descent to Low Town can be made on the cliff railway **Ⓓ** (see box) or by Stoneway Steps. Either way, you can make a slight detour at the bottom to visit Lavington's Hole **Ⓔ**, created during the Civil War, when Royalist forces were besieged in the castle above. A Colonel Lavington was charged with undermining and destroying their munitions dump. However, the resistance of the King's forces was broken in just three weeks, before the sappers' tunnel was completed.

INDUSTRIAL CENTRE

The riverside at Underhill Street was the centre of Bridgnorth's busy river traffic for centuries. The local industries of tanning, weaving, drapery, malting, nailing and an iron foundry were all serviced by the river. Barges or trows were towed upstream by teams of men, later replaced by horses. This trade survived until the coming of the railways; the last barge came downriver in 1895.

The route leaves the town at this point to follow the Severn to Daniel's Mill **Ⓕ**. There was no Daniel; the mill was originally known as Donynges Mill, and this gradually evolved to Dunnings, then Dunnells before acquiring its current name around 1880. The original mill had

▼*Bridgnorth Station has been restored and is once again home to a collection of working steam locomotives.*

▲*Daniel's Mill is a working watermill near the Severn. Behind it is a railway viaduct that was built around 1860.*

line of trees to a waymarked stile. Go straight along the stony lane to where it meets a tarmac road. Turn left, and left again at a T-junction, towards a church.

6 Just before the church, take a waymarked path to your right across a stony parking area. Cross a stile and follow a clear path ahead to a footbridge over the bypass. At the far side turn immediately right to a stile. Go round the left-hand edge of the playing field, before crossing an open space to a stile by

a poplar tree. Cross this and walk down to Bridgnorth Station **Ⓖ**.

7 Follow the tarmac drive left, to the main road by the Hollyhead Inn. Turn left. At a right turn signposted to the Tourist Information Centre, turn sharp right up Ebenezer Steps. Cross West Castle Street at the top, and bear right along Castle Walk, noting the Castle ruins **Ⓗ**. At the end, turn left, then right along the High Street, passing the Town Hall **Ⓙ** and Northgate as you return to the car park.

ALL PHOTOS: ROBERT EAMES

no house attached, and a journey-man miller operated the machinery seasonally. It operated until 1957, grinding grain for animal feed until the death of the miller, the current owner's father. In fact, the mill has been in the hands of the same family for more than 200 years.

RESTORED WATERMILL

Now fully restored, it is open to the public and produces stone-ground bread flour. Its large mill wheel, 38 feet (11.5m) in diameter, was probably made in nearby Coalbrookdale, where the Industrial Revolution began, and was installed in 1855. It is a breast shot wheel; water pours into the buckets at about axle height, so the weight of the filled, descending buckets is effective for about a quarter turn.

The water supply comes from ponds on Potseething Spring, which enters the Severn here. Upstream is a smaller mill, built around 1600 and known locally as 'The Mill in the Hole'. The imposing viaduct over the valley dates from 1860 and carries a restored steam railway.

The walk continues along the river, then loops round on lanes and byways — crossing the railway and the upper reaches of Pot-seething Spring — to head back to Bridgnorth. It returns to the town near Bridgnorth Station **G**, the northern terminus of the Severn Valley Line. The station was opened in 1862 and was a stop on the Great Western line between Shrewsbury and Hartlebury. This line was never profitable, though it had some strategic importance during the war years, and was closed by Dr Beeching in 1963.

BOTH PHOTOS: ROBERT EAMES

▲*Little remains of the castle, which was blown up by gunpowder in 1646.*

Two years later, a preservation society was formed, and steam passenger services were resumed on a section of track in 1970. From 1984, there has been a regular service between Bridgnorth and Kidderminster, 16 miles (25.6km) away, a much longer run than on most restored steam lines. The five stations on the way are fully restored in the best GWR style, with atmospheric touches like period luggage, milk churns and ticket machines.

EXPLOSIVE FINISH

Returning to High Town, there are good views of the ruins of the castle **H** — blown up three months after the end of the siege — and of Panpudding Hill, where Cromwell's forces set up their batteries.

The return walk along the High Street passes the Town Hall **J**, which was completed in 1652, shortly after the end of the Civil War. Bridgnorth suffered considerably in the war, and many public buildings were rebuilt at about this time. The arched ground floor was built in sandstone but later faced with brick. The half-timbered council chambers on the first floor are open to visitors at certain times.

Inland Cliff Railway

Bridgnorth's split-level site is served by many flights of steps. These have always been well-used; a survey in 1890 showed that more than 3,000 people used Stoneway Steps, the main route, in a single day. However, the climb involved more than 200 steps, and as soon as the technology was developed, a cliff railway was built.

Work began on 2 November 1891. A trackway was cut into the cliff, a task complicated by the close proximity of several buildings, and by the discovery of caves in the sandstone that had to be supported with masonry and iron braces. The end result was a cutting 201 feet (61m) long and 111 feet (34m) high. The gradient of 33° was the steepest for any English railway.

Each of the two cars was mounted on a triangular frame that housed a 2,000-gallon (9.1-kl) water tank. The tank belonging to the car at the top station was filled with water from a tank on the station roof; the car was pulled down the track by gravity, in turn pulling up the bottom car, whose discharged water had been pumped back up to the top.

This ingenious method was abandoned in 1944 in favour of an electric winding engine, similar to those used in collieries. Automatic brakes, to lock the cars to the rails if the cable fails, have been duplicated by modern air brakes.

Running between sandstone cliffs, the cliff railway is an alternative to the steps.

◀Field edges and hedge bottoms support poppies, ox-eye daisies and other wild flowers that provide nectar and pollen for the foraging honey bees (inset) from the local hives.

THE EAST

FACT FILE

✳ Burgh le Marsh, 4 miles (6.4km) west of Skegness, on the A158

OS Pathfinder 784 (TF 46/56), grid reference TF 500650

miles 0 1 2 3 4 5 6 7 8 9 10 miles
kms 0 1 2 3 4 5 6 7 8 9 10 11 12 13 14 15 kms

◔ Allow at least 3 hours

▭ Level walking, mostly on good paths and tracks. Some paths through arable fields may be muddy in winter and overgrown in summer

P Free car park at the start

T Nearest BR at Skegness, Tel. (01733) 68181. For details of bus services to Burgh le Marsh, Tel. (01522) 553135

🍺 Several pubs in Burgh le Marsh, and the Red Lion pub in Orby

🍴 Cafés and tea-rooms in Burgh le Marsh

WC In the car park

⌂ Gunby Hall (National Trust) is open Wednesdays, April-September, 2-6pm. The gardens are open Wednesday-Thursday, April-September, 2-6pm (admission charge), Tel. (01909) 486411 for further details

Through a lowland landscape to a 'haunt of ancient peace'

The Lindsey coastal marsh, west of Skegness, is an area of meadows and drainage channels, with farm buildings, hamlets and country houses standing on the relatively high ground. This is a necessary precaution. The whole area has historically been subject to disastrous floods; the most recent of these, in 1953, claimed 43 lives.

This walk visits several small settlements around the marsh, including a country house connected with Alfred, Lord Tennyson. It begins in the centre of Burgh (pronounced 'borough') le Marsh Ⓐ. Chartered fairs and markets were

▶ Field ponds on the route are home to water lilies and other aquatic life.

THE WALK

BURGH LE MARSH – GUNBY – ORBY

The walk starts from the main car park in the centre of Burgh le Marsh ⒶA.

▶ Turn right along the A158 to pass the church ⒷB and the White Swan pub. Beyond a converted windmill, turn left up Elm Crescent. Next to No. 25,

climb the stile and walk diagonally right on the signposted path to the far side of the meadow. At the stile, turn left along the field headland to a road.

▶2 Turn right. After about 100 paces, turn left on a signposted path across 'Billy's Acre'. Climb the stile and follow the hedge

to the far end of the field. Cross a small wooden bridge and follow the wire fence around the right-hand side of a meadow. Cross a stile and a small concrete bridge into an arable field, turn right and follow the headland left towards a farm building. Bear left along a wire fence

around the building. Climb the stile and go straight ahead, through a gate by a bungalow, to a signpost and stile onto a road.

▶3 Cross and go through a metal gate. Walk towards a stile by a tree and hedge almost straight ahead. Cross and continue over the meadows ahead,

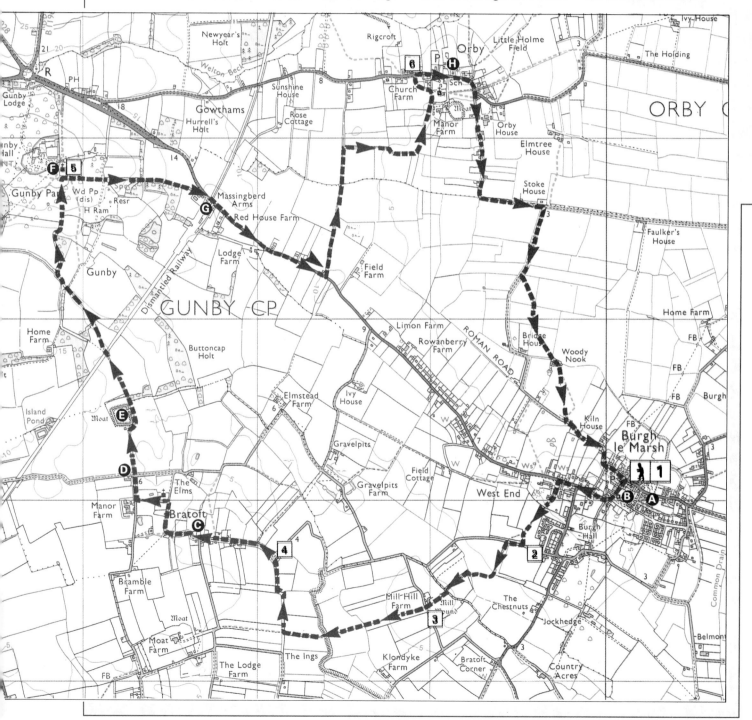

44

crossing a small concrete bridge, to a stile on the far side. Continue over three consecutive concrete bridges to a green lane. Turn right and follow it as it bears left and right to a road by a farmhouse.

4 Turn left and walk through Bratoft C. By the church, turn left along the signposted road to Irby in the Marsh, then go right at Brambleberry Lane (signposted to Firsby and Gunby). At a T-junction by a cottage D, take the signposted footpath straight ahead. At the far end, turn right over a stile, then bear left along the moat E. At the end of the moat, go straight on. Go over a stile and along a headland to the far end of the field. Cross the old railway line and go straight ahead across an arable field onto a waymarked green lane. Where the lane ends, continue across open parkland, following a wire fence on your right. At the end of the fence, climb a waymarked stile and follow the worn path round to the left to a wooden gate. Climb the stile and continue straight ahead to the church F.

5 Take the waymarked path to your right, across the park, over a stile in the hedge and across an arable field to a copse. At the far side of the copse, continue ahead to arrive at a main road. Turn right, passing the former railway station G, and continue for ½ mile (800m). Just beyond a small house, turn left on a signposted bridleway, a gravel track that becomes a green lane. At the end of the lane, continue in the same direction along a headland path for about ¼ mile (400m). Turn right along a track, go through a metal gate and continue ahead to a second gate. Bear right and follow the hedge on your left around the edge of the meadow. At the far end, turn left through a wooden gate and cross the field towards the church. Continue ahead to two stiles in the corner. Do not climb these, but turn left and walk alongside the wire fence behind the houses. Climb the stile and take a path between the houses to a road.

6 Turn right through Orby H to the junction by the Red Lion pub. Follow the road signposted to Burgh le Marsh as it bends left, then right. About ¼ mile (400m) beyond the right bend, take a signposted path to your left. Walk diagonally across an arable field. Cross a bridge by a waymark and go straight ahead, across another field and a small bridge, to the far end of a farmhouse. Cross the concrete bridge. Go diagonally left across a field to a metalled road. Turn left and follow it back into Burgh le Marsh.

---

held here from 1400 to the end of the 19th century, and the Market Place has many fine Georgian and Victorian buildings.

The site's history stretches far back into antiquity. Stone Age flint tools have been found near Cock Hill, a grassy mound by the church that is believed to have been used for Saxon burials and was converted into a cockpit in the Middle Ages. Not far from here, a ferry across the Wash linked up with an important Roman road, the Peddar's Way.

There are some interesting buildings, including three old hostelries — the Fleece Inn, The Bell Hotel and The White Swan pub — and two windmills. One of these, a five-storey, five-sailed tower mill built in 1833, is in full working order.

On its way out of town, the route passes the Church of St Peter and St Paul B, a handsome Perpendicular building with a carved Jacobean pulpit. Its tall tower of Portland stone functioned as a landmark to ships far out in the North Sea.

SYMBOLIC PAINTING

You walk over meadows and pastures, across dykes and along lanes to Bratoft C. The village church, also dedicated to St Peter and St Paul, has a tower dating from 1747. Inside the tower is a strange painting on wood depicting the Spanish Armada as a red dragon, which is threatening the little English fleet and the army massed along the coast.

On the outskirts of the village is an old lodge D, whose projecting first-floor bay window is supported on timbers. Just beyond is the moated site of the original seat of the Massingberd family. The house was demolished in 1698, though the remnants of a brick bridge across the moat E still survive.

The Massingberds' subsequent

▲The path crosses grazed parkland on the way to Gunby Hall. The old station of Burgh le Marsh (below) was much nearer the hall than it was the village.

◄Wheat and other crops flourish on the rich alluvial soil of the drained marsh.

ALL PHOTOS: JASON SMALLEY

home lies a little to the north. Gunby Hall (see box) with 1,400 acres (567 hectares) of park and farmland, was presented to the National Trust in 1944 by the last of the family line.

In the park, near the hall's charming walled garden, is a church **F**. Rebuilt in 1870, it contains two 15th-century brasses to the Massingberd family. An 18th-century coach house is topped by a clocktower brought here from Hampshire in 1917.

A little way beyond the exit from the parkland is the former railway station **G** of Burgh le Marsh, nearly 2 miles (3.2km) from the town centre. A bus from the Bell Hotel used to meet all the trains here.

The line that ran through the station was part of the East Lincoln-shire Railway, which was set up with local cash in 1848 (towards the end of the 'railway mania' boom). The track was leased to the Great Northern Railway.

STEPPING OVER THE LINE

By 1890, there were six trains each weekday to Peterborough, and through trains from Grimsby and London began to call at the station at the beginning of the century. It was also a well used goods line, with animal feed, coal, fertilizer and fish being brought in, and hay, sugar beet and potatoes being taken out.

The line became part of the LNER under the 1923 Amalgamation Act,

▲*The village church at Orby is a long building with a tower, parts of which date from the 13th century.*

was used for armoured trains for coastal defences in World War II. The station, closed in 1970 but reopened 17 years later as the Lincolnshire Railway Museum, has unfortunately since had to be sold along with its exhibits.

From the station, another walk across the meadows leads to Orby **H**, a wooded village on the edge of the marsh. Its 13th-century church stands among the trees and there is an attractive vicarage and an old brick manor house.

From Orby, the route heads back towards Burgh le Marsh. The town's church tower dominates the wide horizon ahead as you follow lanes along old embankments, just above the low-lying, marshy fields.

▼*The well preserved five-sailed windmill at Burgh le Marsh.*

Gunby Hall

The house, its gardens and the surrounding parkland have been managed by the National Trust since 1944.

The main three-storey house dates from 1700, with the north wing having been added in 1873. The entrance faces west, and nearly all the windows in the south end are blank. The rose-coloured red-brick front is a good example of a typical house of William III's reign. Some of the bricks are thought to have come from Bratoft Hall, the previous home of the Massingberds, and to have originated from Holland. Most, however, probably came from a local brickyard.

Nearly all the wainscoting in the interior is of the simplest kind, with large panels. The staircase is the hall's most elaborate internal feature. In the west drawing room hang portraits by Joshua Reynolds of Bennet Langton and Mary, his wife. Manuscript pages of Tennyson's poetry hang in the hall at Gunby, with his signature and the date 1849; the lines 'a haunt of ancient peace' were composed, according to tradition, with Gunby in mind.

The gardens were mostly laid out early in the 19th century by Elizabeth Langton Massingberd, and in about 1900 by Stephen and Margaret Massingberd. The gardens, with their mixture of vegetables, fruit and flowers, are one of the chief attractions at the hall.

The hall was built by Sir William Massingberd, the second baronet. The site was previously occupied by a small manor house built by a family called Gunby; only a few traces of the original manor still exist.

Sir William Massingberd died in 1719. His son, also Sir William, died unmarried in 1723 and the direct line of the family became extinct. Since then, the property, and the name, have descended through female lines.

In the 18th century, the Langtons of Langton married into the Massingberd family. In Boswell's biography of Dr Johnson, Bennet Langton is noted as a friend of the great man. Among the hall's treasures is an autographed copy of the first edition of the *Life of Dr Johnson*. Only six such copies are known to survive, and this is the only one still in Britain.

ALL PHOTOS: JASON SMALLEY

EIGHT SAILS TO THE WIND

THE EAST

NEIL HOLMES. INSET: STEPHEN DALTON/N·H·PA

FACT FILE

⚹ Heckington, 5 miles (8km) south-east of Sleaford, on the A17

▭ Pathfinder 815 (TF 04/14), grid reference TF 145435

miles 0 1 2 3 4 5 6 7 8 9 10 miles
kms 0 1 2 3 4 5 6 7 8 9 10 11 12 13 14 15 kms

🕐 Allow at least 2 hours

▬ Mostly level walking on metalled lanes and pavements. Some field paths, which may be muddy

P Free car park at the start

T BR mainline service, Tel. (01733) 68181. Various bus services, Tel. (01522) 553135 for details

🍺 Several pubs in Heckington. Café at Pearoom Craft Centre

WC At the start

⌂ Heckington Windmill is open all year except Christmas and New Year, Tel. (01529) 60765 for days and times

Explore a Fenland village with a unique windmill

Heckington boasts the only surviving eight-sailed windmill in England, a lovely church with a richly-carved Easter sepulchre, and several other fine buildings. This walk explores this small jewel of a village and its setting in the Fens, crossed here by the line of one of the first canals built in Britain.

The route begins at the Pearoom

▲*Great Hale Fen, once a marshy wilderness, has been drained to create fertile farmland. The great ramshorn snail (inset) is a freshwater snail that occurs in Fenland dykes and ditches.*

Craft Centre Ⓐ. This building dates from 1870, and until 1961 it was used as a warehouse for sorting peas. Subsequently renovated by the Heckington Village Trust, it now includes craft workshops as well as a gallery with displays of work

▼*The Pearoom is one of several renovated buildings in Heckington.*

NEIL HOLMES

THE WALK

HECKINGTON – GREAT HALE

The walk starts from the car park at the Pearoom Craft Centre Ⓐ, where the B1394 crosses the railway line.

▶ 1 Turn left along the Hale road, and continue over the level crossing, with the windmill Ⓑ on your right. Follow the road for ¼ mile (400m).

▶ 2 Just after the village sign on your right for Heckington, turn left down a tarmac path running behind bungalows, then bear right along Queens Road. At a T-junction, turn left. Turn right down Kings Lane, then left along a passage into the High Street. Turn right. Immediately beyond the post office, turn left down Chapel Lane to a T-junction.

▶ 3 Take the signposted path to the left of a barn with a corrugated-metal roof, and follow it along a dyke on your right, eventually crossing under a power line, with a pylon on your left. Where the dyke ends, continue ahead towards a single tree, then turn left for a short way to a ditch. Turn right and follow the ditch for just over ¼ mile (400m) to where a dyke crosses at right angles. Beyond the dyke, head diagonally right across the field to a signpost by a white bridge.

▶ 4 Turn left down the metalled road and follow it for 2 miles (3.2km), crossing the course of Car Dyke Ⓒ and two level crossings over the railway Ⓓ, back to Great Hale.

▶ 5 Beyond Rookery Farm, turn right, signposted 'Little Hale ½ mile', and continue to Queens Road. Turn right to retrace your steps to the Hale road. Continue past the Pearoom to a crossroads. Turn left into the High Street to the Nag's Head Ⓔ. Walk diagonally across the green past the almshouses Ⓕ, and turn right along Church Street to St Andrews Ⓖ. Go right along St Andrews Street, past Church House Ⓗ on your right, then right again down Eastgate. Continue ahead at the crossroads to return to the start of the walk.

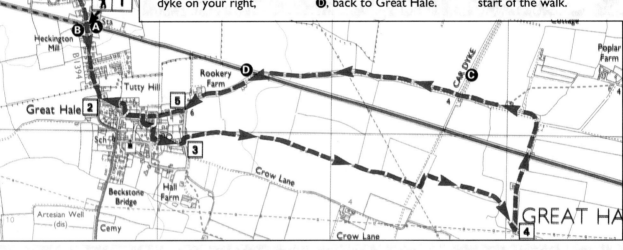

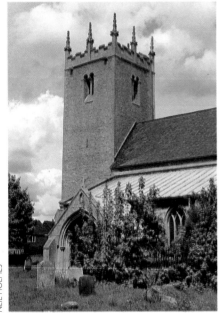

from all over the county.

Just over the railway from the craft centre is Heckington's unique windmill Ⓑ (see box), which you pass on the way to the village of Great Hale. The village church, which once belonged to nearby Bardney Abbey, lost its chancel in the middle of the 17th century, but remains a striking building with long aisles and a spacious porch.

SAXON ORIGINS

Its rugged tower is Saxon, dating to perhaps a century before the Norman Conquest. There are two notable, 17th-century memorials.

◀ *Great Hale's church has Saxon bell openings; it was owned by Bardney Abbey, 18 miles (28.8km) to the north.*

One shows a Robert Cawdron and his 21 children, and the other another Robert Cawdron, presumably one of the 21, who died in 1665, the year of the Great Plague.

ANCIENT CANAL

The walk out onto Great Hale Fen crosses the line of Car Dyke Ⓒ. Along with the Fosdyke, this is the only Roman-built canal in Britain. The first known reference to it was in the Danelaw Charters, where it is called Karesdic, the ditch of Kari, although its origins clearly predate the Danes. Archaeologists disagree as to whether it was a purpose-built canal or a large catchwater drain that was also used for transport.

As in many places along its length, silting here has reduced it to

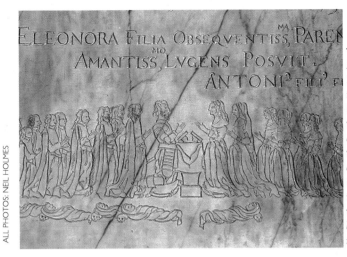

◀*Inside Great Hale's church is this 17th-century memorial to Robert Cawdron and his wife, with their 21 children, five of whom died in childhood. Car Dyke (below) was an important Roman waterway but has become badly silted up in many places.*

wanted to get to Sleaford that there was no room on the train; when the Station Master refused to reimburse the fares of the disappointed passengers there was a riot.

LONG EXCURSION

Every Feast Wednesday, all the children from the local Sunday schools went on a special excursion train to Skegness. The train was so long that it had to stop twice at every station so that passengers were able to get on and off.

an insignificant drain. However, it originally ran for some 56 miles (90km) from the Nene, east of Peterborough, to the Witham, just south of Lincoln, where it marks the western boundary of the Fens. Its character varies along its length; parts appear to follow the natural land form, while other sections of it are clearly man-made.

OVER THE LINE

The return route follows Great Hale Drove, one of the ancient routes across the Fen. This road twice crosses the railway line to Heckington. Laid in 1857 by the Boston, Sleaford and Midland Counties Railway, the line was soon taken over by the Great Northern Railway. It is now part of the BR line that runs between Nottingham and

◀*The station buildings at Heckington, including the signal box (left), which was built in the 1880s, have been restored by the Heckington Village Trust.*

Skegness via Grantham.

The route returns to Heckington Station ❶, which was opened in 1859 and modified in 1882-4, when the signal box was built by the GNR. The buildings fell into disrepair, but were taken over and restored by the Heckington Village Trust in 1975.

THE RAILWAY HOTEL

The line, originally a single track, brought increased prosperity to the village. The Railway Hotel was built in 1860, and the GNR built the Pearoom, with a branch line leading right up to the building, as a speculative venture.

The railway was enormously popular in its early years. One market day in 1861, so many people

The centre of old Heckington lies to the north of the railway. The village is recorded in the *Domesday Book* (1083) as Echintune, and was held at that time by Gilbert de Gaunt under the Crown.

HIGH TREASON

The only time it appears in national history after that was in the time of James I when Henry, 9th Lord Cobham of Heckington, and his brother, George, were convicted of high treason. George was executed, but Lord Cobham was reprieved; he died in poverty in 1619.

The Nag's Head ❷, in the High Street, lays claim to having once numbered the highwayman Dick Turpin among its overnight guests. This is not inconceivable; at his trial in 1739, Turpin was convicted of stealing a mare and foal from Heckington Common.

Across the green is a group of

◄The Nag's Head in Heckington, where Dick Turpin is reputed to have stayed in the early 18th century; the inn still offers overnight accommodation.

The exterior features a handsome corbel-table and some splendid gargoyles. The nave, chancel and transepts all have large windows with geometric tracery, while the well-proportioned tower is topped by a handsome spire.

EASTER SEPULCHRE

Inside, there is a fine tomb belonging to Richard de Pottesgrave, who was Chaplain to Edward II and Edward III and paid for the building of the chancel. Probably the church's greatest treasure is its Easter sepulchre, widely considered among the best in England, which is wonderfully well carved.

Not far from the church, and on the other side of St Andrews Street, is Church House ❶, a former Wesleyan chapel that now houses a permanent exhibition detailing the history of the church. From here, it is an easy walk through the village back to the Pearoom.

Gothic almshouses ❶, erected in 1888 as a result of a bequest by one Henry Godson. In 1905, four more were built by the church thanks to the generosity of his kinsman, Edward Godson.

The church itself ❶, dedicated to St Andrew, is one of the finest in the county. It is the third church to have been built on this site. Almost all of it dates from the 13th and 14th centuries and it is in the Decorated style — for many, the finest form of Gothic architecture — throughout.

Heckington's Windmill

There has been a windmill in the village of Heckington since Michael Hare built a five-sailed model in 1830. It was not widely used, and changed hands several times before a thunderstorm damaged it in 1890. The sails broke off and the iron castings of the brake wheel, windshaft and cross were destroyed, and the mill was abandoned.

Two years later, its owner, a Mr Nash, met John Pocklington, who had bought a redundant mill with eight sails at Skirbeck, near Boston, and the two men made a deal. Skirbeck mill was stripped and its parts put into the stricken tower at Heckington, where Pocklington set up a bakery and milling business.

At first this venture was reasonably successful, but commercial pressures brought a gradual decline, and operations ceased in 1946. The sails and cap were removed in 1951 and the mill began to decay. Recognizing the importance of the building,

Kesteven Council bought it for £2,000 in 1953 and began to restore it. Since 1973 it has been administered by Lincolnshire County Council, and was restored to working order in 1986.

The first windmill to have more than four sails was designed by John Smeaton in 1758, and erected at Leeds. No more than 40 or so were built, and only seven of those had as many as eight sails. The only surviving example of this type is that at Heckington.

Each pair of sails spans a diameter of 70 feet (21m). At optimum grinding speed the tips move at 25mph (40kmh). They are fitted to a cap that revolves on top of a six-storey, 60-foot (18-m) brick tower; a fantail on the back of the cap keeps them pointed into the wind.

The eight sails, which came from Tuxford's Mill in Skirbeck, have a sail area of over 1500 square feet (139 sq m). The mill has five pairs of stones on three floors.

NEIL HOLMES.INSET: STEPHEN DALTON/NHPA

▲*Thursford Church, partially hidden by trees, can be seen across the lush fields from Clark's Lane. A barn owl (left) effortlessly carries off its prey after a hard night's hunting.*

Old Crawfish Inn and Forge **B** still stand by the route and further on is their later counterpart, the Victorian Crawfish Inn **D**, built to service the railway, which closed in 1959. The past glories of the steam age can be relived by visiting the Thursford Collection at the end of the walk.

Around a pretty village deep in the heart of Norfolk

Thursford would normally be a very sleepy village, were it not for the fact that it is home to the Thursford Collection **A**, a fascinating museum of all kinds of steam engines, and mechanical organs. The collection was started by George Cushing, who owned a road rolling

business in Thursford in the 1930s and collected steam engines. Today the collection includes a narrow-gauge steam railway, a gondola roundabout, many beautiful old steam road and showmen's engines, as well as a collection of extravagantly decorated mechanical organs and the mighty Wurlitzer organ, all of which give musical shows. There is a Victorian shopping arcade, various kinds of refreshments and a free car park and picnic area.

The walk leaves the village and continues along a green lane to the main road which used to be a busy coaching route. The 15th-century

NEIL HOLMES

◀*One of the many working mechanical organs at the Thursford Collection.*

FACT FILE

✳	Thursford, Norfolk
🗺	Pathfinder 840 (TF 83/93), grid reference TF 981344

miles 0   1   2   3   4   5   6   7   8   9   10 miles
kms 0 1 2 3 4 5 6 7 8 9 10 11 12 13 14 15 kms

🕐	1½ hours
▬	Can be muddy in places
P	The Thursford Collection car park in the village or Thursford village green nearby
🏛🍴	At the Thursford Collection, the Old Crawfish Forge and the Crawfish Inn on the A148
I	Thursford Collection, Tel. Thursford (01328) 878477

THE WALK

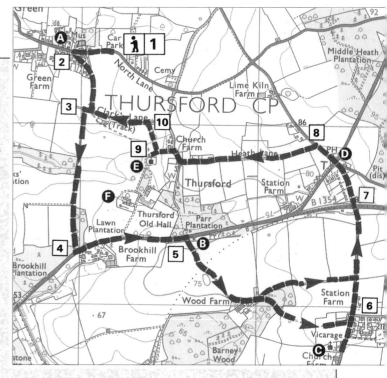

THURSFORD – BARNEY

The walk begins at the Thursford Collection **A** car park.

1 Turn right out of the car park and walk along the road to Thursford Green.

2 Turn left here down Clark's Lane past cottages on the right and a Dutch gabled house on the left. The lane turns into a broad stony track. Keep ahead along this between hedges and trees to reach a T-junction of tracks and turn right a short way.

3 The path then turns left and passes for some distance through fields with a view of the church **E** and Old Hall **F** over on the left. Continue on through a grove of poplars and over a stream then through woodland to meet the busy A148 Fakenham to Cromer Road.

4 Turn left along this, walking on the broad verge. On the left are more views of the Old Hall. Pass a track leading to the Old Coach House (farm holidays) and then cross the road carefully to a petrol station. Just beyond the petrol station are the Old Crawfish Inn and Forge **B**.

5 Walk between the buildings just to the right of the pumps and cross a stile on the boundary behind (marked with an arrow) into a field. Walk ahead down the field edge along a slightly raised bank to meet a stile just to the left of a small stretch of hedge by a farm gate. Cross this and walk to the left along a farm track by a pantiled barn on the left. Bear left at another farm track (more farm buildings on the right). Here take an easy concessionary route to avoid crops by walking left down the farm track to the road. Turn right here to reach Barney church **C**. Alternatively, just by cottages on the left, take the marked track to the right through woodland. This comes out into a field with the church visible ahead. Walk slightly to the left across the middle of the field towards houses beyond a stretch of hedge. Turn right along this hedge and follow the field edge, left then right by houses to emerge onto the road through a gap. Turn right to visit the church.

6 Turn back along the road and walk past houses and then Station Farm on the right. Continue past the signpost to Wood Farm where the concessionary route comes out, and carry on to a T-junction.

7 Cross the B1354 here and go ahead past bungalows to a crossroads. Cross over to the Victorian Crawfish Inn **D** and walk along the lane signposted to Thursford Green.

8 Before long turn left onto tiny flowery Heath Lane and continue on to some old cottages on the right. Bear right just past these then left down a stony track to reach Thursford church. For a closer look at the Old Hall **F** turn left out of the church down the track.

9 Leave the church and turn right down the track a little way. Just by the bottom of a garden, turn left up a broad grassy track at the side of a field.

10 At the top of the field turn left along another broad track. At a junction of tracks just past a modern barn on the left, turn right to return to Thursford Green.

NEIL HOLMES

▲ *This pretty dovecote tower sits in a former walled vegetable garden in the grounds of Thursford Old Hall.*

The only notable building in Barney on the next stage of the walk is St Mary's church **C**; it is Early English with some Perpendicular work. It has a 16th-century tower and a 15th-century chapel and nave.

PASTORAL SETTING

The walk returns to Thursford along a tiny, flowery lane which leads to St Andrew's church **E** in its pastoral setting near the Elizabethan 'big house', Thursford Old Hall **F**. All that remains of this Tudor manor, which was mostly demolished in 1918, is the huge kitchen area with its ornate Tudor chimneys. The church is adorned on the south side with four demon gargoyles. The north door is 13th century, with some fine ironwork. Under the tower are some monuments dating back to 1666, mainly commemorating the Guybon family who owned Thursford Hall in Tudor times. This exceptional church was restored in the 19th century and contains many fine examples of good Victorian workmanship including the font, the pulpit, the chancel and some lovely stained glass. The elevated south chapel, which stands over the Chad family vault, was once the Chad family pew. They owned Thursford Hall from 1653 until the beginning of this century.

NORFOLK NATURE WALK

A varied walk through woodland and common to the north Norfolk coast

This walk includes much that is special about the north Norfolk coast, an Area of Outstanding Natural Beauty with a uniquely haunting atmosphere. Wide sea views, a range of local and migrant birds and a profusion of wild flowers, in a woodland and common setting, are all to be seen. The walk also takes in Roman Camp on Beacon Hill, the highest point in Norfolk, Runton, once the target of pirates, and Sheringham, a busy little resort which has grown up around an old fishing village and boasts some of the country's finest beaches as well as a full-size steam passenger railway, The Poppy Line.

FACT FILE

- ✴ Pretty Corner, situated on the north Norfolk coast, 5 miles (8km) west of Cromer, off the A148

- 🚗 Pathfinder 820 (TG 04/14), grid reference TG 155411

  miles 0 1 2 3 4 5 6 7 8 9 10 miles
  kms 0 1 2 3 4 5 6 7 8 9 10 11 12 13 14 15 kms

- ◔ Allow 5 hours

- ▭ Easy, along good tracks and paths. Walkable the whole year round

- P Free parking in the woodland car park at Pretty Corner

- 🍴 Pretty Corner Restaurant at the start, a café/shop at Roman Camp, and at West Runton a seaside café and toilets close to beach
- WC

▲ *View to Beeston Bump across poppy-clad farmland. (inset) The kittiwake breeds on the coast.*
▼ *The North Norfolk Railway runs steam trains between Sheringham and Holt.*

53

THE WALK

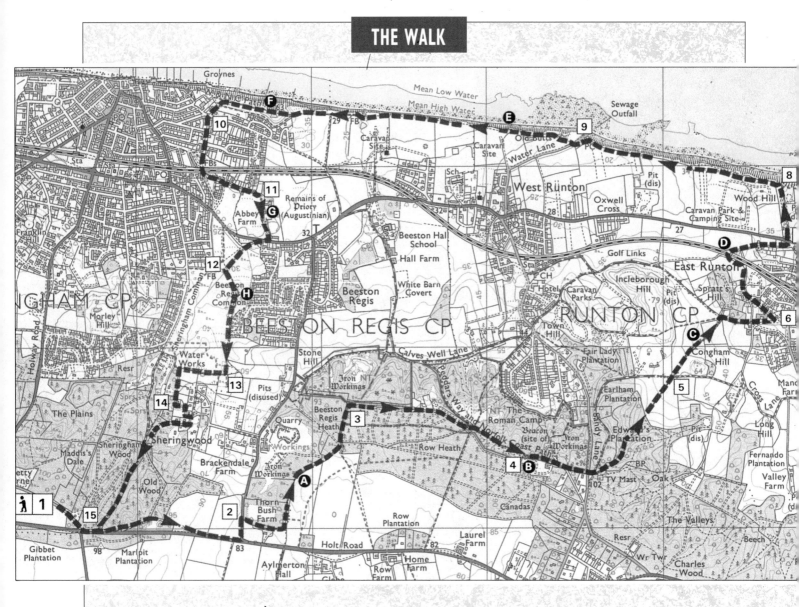

PRETTY CORNER — EAST RUNTON — SHERINGHAM

The walk begins at the car park at Pretty Corner.

▶ From the information board in the car park go left into the wood. Follow paths signposted to tea rooms, always taking right forks, then turn right to the road. Turn left and, at main road, turn left into minor road, passing café on left. At main road turn left, walking along wide grass verge. Turn left again into minor road, rejoin main road for a short distance, then turn left into road signposted for Beeston Regis.

▶ Turn right off road at edge of woodland, following green bridleway sign. Follow a fence on your left which bends sharply left after a short distance. Turn left and continue to the end of the field on your right and another sharp left bend in the fence. Ignore paths to your right and follow the fence on your left through the wood **Ⓐ**.

▶ Just before junction of paths where fence on left again goes sharp left, turn sharply right a short distance along a path to a crossing of paths. Turn left along wide path, ignoring all other paths. Pass a flint house on left with fine views over the coast. Eventually the path bends sharply left and ends in a wide, stony track opposite a cairn. Turn right and this main woodland track passes a caravan park on right before arriving at Roman Camp **Ⓑ** with its heritage board.

▶ From the heritage board keep the café/shop on right and continue to a fork. Ignore path to right and go on to meet a road. Cross road and continue along woodland track, taking the middle one with 'no horse rides' and 'footpath' signs. This path goes downhill, then through an arable field.

▶ Keeping camp site on left at cross paths, go along middle path between fields **Ⓒ**. At next junction of paths take right-hand path downhill under overhanging hedges to a road on the edge of East Runton Common by a flint wall. Turn left along metalled road to a junction.

▶ Turn left up metalled lane between a hedge and brick houses. The lane becomes a rough track with a caravan park and then a railway cutting on right. Turn right over railway bridge **Ⓓ** and continue along track with Forge Cottage on right. Continue downhill to road.

▶ Cross main road slightly leftwards and take the

VIEWPOINTS

Soon after its start the walk goes through natural woodland **A**. Many plants grow beside the path, including rosebay willowherb, bluebells, herb-robert, campion and foxgloves, depending on the season.

Roman Camp **B** is 350 feet (105 metres) above sea level, one of the highest points in Norfolk, and offers extensive views of the coastline. It has been used as a beacon for centuries and formed part of a coastal warning system. Runton was at one time considered to be one of the most dangerous places on the Norfolk coast. A watch was kept here as early as 1324, not only for invaders, but also for pirates who roamed the coastline. Despite

Upper Sheringham was once a busy agricultural area. Only the disproportionately large church and churchyard reveal its lost importance.

▲ *Beeston Regis Common is an unspoilt wildlife habitat. Its ponds, plants and trees attract dragonflies, butterflies and birds. (above) The ruins of 13th-century Beeston priory are a haunting reminder of the contemplative life.*

ABOVE AND INSET PAUL FELIX

DEREK FORSS

grassy path with footpath sign to the coast.

8 Turn left along the cliff path which overlooks lovely sandy beaches. This is a permissive route subject to continual erosion. It is safer to keep inside the fence which goes along the edge of caravan parks at times.

9 At West Runton cross the beach road and go through car park, keeping to the left, to rejoin the coastal path **E**. About ¾ mile (1200 metres) further on, after passing the last caravan park, go over a narrow path crossing a stream. A public footpath continues along the coast. Ignore the path to the left. Go up the steep hill via the steps to the top of

Beeston Bump **F**, a marvellous viewpoint, with views inland and along the coast. Leaving the Bump, keep to the path away from the coast and close to the houses. Ignore path to right and continue down the narrow path to some iron railings.

10 Cross road and go along Curtis Lane. Just after the railway bridge turn left on to path over common. This path then goes between stream and houses. Continue straight ahead along metalled path between houses and common. The path becomes a rough track. Ignore lane to the left.

11 Turn right at footpath

sign, passing a ruined priory **G** on left. At main road turn right, then left into a lay-by. Halfway along the lay-by turn left on to footpath over Beeston Regis Common **H** with its wealth of wild flowers.

12 At the pond turn squarely left at a junction of paths and take the one going away from the houses. Ignore all paths to left and right. The correct path passes the back of bungalows on its left, then goes under an avenue of trees. Continue along the path and where it divides take the left-hand fork.

13 At the gate keep right, then head left to rejoin the main path. Ignore paths to right and at T-junction turn

left. This path becomes a rough track running between houses.

14 Turn left and continue round bends to T-junction of tracks by a post box in Sheringwood. Turn right along Robin Hill. Keep along rough track between houses. The path narrows and goes straight ahead into a wood. The route now continues through woodland, going uphill. Ignore paths to right. Cross main path and follow narrow path uphill to road.

15 At the main road turn right, then right again into a minor road signposted Pretty Corner and walk back to the start of the walk at the car park.

Pebbles have been used in Norfolk buildings since the 16th century. These typical cottages display patterns created by pebbles and brickwork.

Fruits of the Sea

Fishing has been a mainstay of the East Anglian economy since time immemorial. The North Sea's rich yield of oysters, crabs, lobsters, whelks and herring was enjoyed by the Romans; indeed, the oysters found such favour with Julius Caesar that he shipped vast quantities back to Italy.

The local fishermen, once known as 'shannocks', still put to sea in the early hours of the morning, returning by breakfast time with their catch, but they are a rarer breed these days as most of the local population is involved in tourism. Nonetheless, the colourful fishing boats can still be seen drawn up on the beach, and Norfolk's reputation for fine sea produce is undimmed. Locals and visitors alike have good reason for hoping it remains so.

its name, there is no evidence that the Romans camped here. Nevertheless, Roman finds have been dug up in the area. There is also evidence of a smelting and ironworks dating from Saxon, Norman and medieval times.

At the edge of the arable fields **C**, there are fine views of the coast and, closer by, many wild flowers. In particular, look for field pansies, bladder campion, Jack-go-to-bed-at-noon, toadflax and green alkanet.

The railway line **D** is the British Rail line from Cromer, which links up with the North Norfolk Railway line at Sheringham. From Sheringham, where there is also a railway museum, several interesting steam locomotives take passengers through beautiful countryside to Weybourne and the little market town of Holt.

COASTAL BIRD LIFE

The coastal path **E** is a good place to watch local and migrating birds, such as the purple sandpiper, great black-backed gull, kittiwake, guillemot and shag. Terns can be seen diving for fish in the sea.

At the triangulation point on top of Beeston Bump **F** there are panoramic views of the coast and countryside, with the seaside town of

▲ *The north Norfolk coast, swept by powerful tides and east winds, has miles of long, straight beaches.*
▼ *The village of Sheringham has been a popular tourist resort since the advent of the railway.*

Sheringham to the west.

Soon after, you will come to the ruins of an Augustinian priory **G** founded in 1216, while Beeston Common **H**, has ponds, trees, and wildflowers, including orchids and monkey flowers. It is worth lingering here as there is so much to see. The flowers naturally attract many species of butterfly and birds.

SECRET VALLEY

▲ *Chappel Viaduct is 1,000 feet (300 metres) long and contains 1,000,000 bricks. (inset) The cormorant, usually a coastal bird, also nests near rivers.*

FACT FILE

⚹ Chappel and Wakes Colne, Essex, 8 miles (12.8 km) north-west of Colchester on A604

▭ Pathfinder 1076 (TL82) and 1077 (TL 92/TM02), grid reference TL 897289

miles 0 1 2 3 4 5 6 7 8 9 10 miles
kms 0 1 2 3 4 5 6 7 8 9 10 11 12 13 14 15 kms

🕐 Allow 2½ hours

▭ Easy, but some dense undergrowth in summer

Ⓟ The East Anglian Railway Museum has given permission to use its car park at front of Wakes Colne station

🍴 Shoulder of Mutton pub at Fordstreet, snacks at station

Ⓣ British Rail branch line from Colchester to Sudbury serves Chappel and Wakes Colne

A secluded riverside and woodland walk in the heart of Essex

Long renowned for its rivers and marshes, Essex also boasts some of the loveliest English countryside. This riverside walk through the Colne valley presents the county at its best.

Starting from the East Anglian Railway Museum car park, the walk passes cottages Ⓐ which were built to house the railway construction workers. After crossing the branch line there are fields and beautifully secluded valleys nestling at the foot of low hills.

ANCIENT ROUTE

Passing through woodland to higher ground beyond Bretts Farm Ⓑ there are extensive views over the Colne valley to the south. The walk then follows an ancient sunken lane past grassy horse paddocks as it descends to Fordstreet Ⓒ.

Then follows the most delightful stretch: past a wall with a variety of flowers growing in it (the real meaning of wallflowers), and on

past a tree and shrub nursery leading to a fine track beside the River Colne Ⓓ. Here you will see water lilies, skylarks, cormorants and a variety of waterfowl. In the distance, the 32-arch Chappel Viaduct Ⓕ is etched tall against the sky.

FINE BUILDINGS

Heading back towards the start, the walk passes through flax country Ⓔ — a rippling expanse of blue in summer. A shrub-lined path leads under the viaduct past a well-stocked duck pond to a fine group of houses and the church of St Barnabas Ⓖ, built here to serve the people who, in days past, found the trek to church in Great Tey too far.

At the end of the walk visit the East Anglian Railway Museum Ⓗ and its excellent bookshop (open all year, except Christmas Day). It operates steam-hauled passenger trains on the first Sunday of each month from Easter to October, and every Sunday in August. The museum points out that this is a working railway and visitors should not walk beside or along the track.

The River Colne meanders past rich farmland, arable fields and woodland for much of its route to the North Sea.

THE WALK

WAKES COLNE – FORDSTREET – CHAPPEL

The walk starts at the East Anglian Railway Museum car park outside Wakes Colne station.

1 Turn right on road outside car park and walk past cottages on left **A**. Take first road on right, cross bridge and turn left beside railway line. At corner turn right beside stream to road. Cross to footpath sign and follow stream, still on left. In corner cross bridge on left, go ahead and turn right through gate. Continue beside hedges and through two more gates.

2 Beyond third gate turn left by water trough on obvious track and fork left uphill through woodland to gate with house ahead. Before gate turn left through another gate and proceed with wood on left. On reaching the field follow the fence on right, crossing it at single tree on right. Turn right and follow line of trees on left to a road at Bretts Farm **B**. Cross and continue along field edge with farm to right.

3 Go over earth bridge, narrow field and ditch to pass through crossing hedge. Turn right, keeping hedge on right and in next corner go through hedge. Turn left, then right at corner for about 35 yards (32 metres). Turn left over earth bridge to reach road.

4 Turn right for 250 yards (225 metres), then enter field on left by footpath sign. Go ahead beside road and turn left in field corner. Follow sunken lane and in corner turn left beside stream for 175 yards (155 metres). Cross stile and bridge, and go through gate on left. Turn right uphill beside fence to stile in crossing hedge. Beyond stile and ditch turn right up bank and through rails to follow hedge on right.

5 In corner turn left for 10 yards (9 metres), then right over narrow bridge and fence rails. Go downhill beside hedge to corner and turn left beside fence (do not cut corner). Turn right through double gates, then left beside hedge and through two railed fences. In corner turn right beside road, and at fence by electricity pole turn left over bridge, then right into road. Very shortly turn left over ditch through gap and turn right on field edge behind houses. Go through crossing hedge and at notice about East Anglian Rides turn right through Shoulder of Mutton car park to reach road **C**.

6 Turn left over bridge, then almost immediately right between low fence and wall by footpath sign. Follow path past nursery. Bear right, then left beside river. At end of first field join a path that later becomes a permissive track **D**.

7 Follow track beside river. At second left bend go ahead to stile. (Ignore bridge on right and track ahead beside river.) Cross stile and go ahead with hedge and pillbox on right.

8 Cross further stile and at hedge corner go ahead over field to deep ditch **E**. Turn left to earth bridge on right (at end of house garden), cross and follow hedge to footpath sign at corner of garden. Turn left to drive and go ahead. Path soon goes through hedge on right, but stay on Popes Lane to railway bridge and turn right to follow the permissive path which runs beside the embankment.

9 At end of field turn left over stile and right on fenced path. This leads left under the viaduct **F** to Chappel village **G**. Turn right on road past the Swan pub, over main road and ahead to car park at museum **H** where the walk started.

THE LINE TO ALLY PALLY

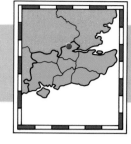

15

THE SOUTH EAST

DAVID HUGHES. INSET: FRANK GREENAWAY/BRUCE COLEMAN LTD

Walking to a hilltop palace along an old railway line

This is a gentle stroll along the track bed of the railway that once linked Finsbury Park and Alexandra Palace. The land has survived threats from developers to become the Parkland Walk, a green and tranquil corridor through the heart of residential north London.

The walk joins two sections of old track bed, via an exploration of Queen's Wood and Highgate Wood, and ends with a short section through a public park to the magnificent hilltop site of Alexandra Palace, which affords fabulous views over London. All along the old track, and in the two woods, the flora and fauna are surprisingly abundant and varied.

Initially, the track bed cuts between Finsbury Park and the busy Intercity line north from King's Cross. The old railway ran from Finsbury Park to Highgate and was opened by the Great Northern

---

FACT FILE

- ✳ Finsbury Park in north London
- ⊡ Pathfinders 1159 (TQ 28/38) and 1140 (TQ 29/39), grid reference TQ 313868

| miles 0 | 1 | 2 | 3 | 4 | 5 | 6 | 7 | 8 | 9 | 10 miles |
| kms 0 | 1 2 | 3 4 | 5 6 7 | 8 9 10 | 11 12 | 13 14 15 kms |

- ◑ Allow at least 2 hours
- ▬ Mostly level tracks with some slightly muddy sections after rain. A couple of very short climbs
- P Some parking in streets near station but watch for parking restrictions
- T BR trains, underground (Victoria and Piccadilly lines) and buses to Finsbury Park Station. Return to station by bus
- 🍴 Pubs at Highgate and Alexandra Palace. Cafés in Highgate Wood and The Grove
- WC At Highgate Wood and Alexandra Palace

▲*Alexandra Palace, which has burned down twice since being opened in 1873, sits on a hill at the northern end of the walk. Natterer's bat (inset) has been recently seen at Highgate Wood.*

Railway in 1867; the branch line from Highgate to Alexandra Palace was opened in 1873.

The line was taken over by the London and North Eastern Railway in 1923, by which time it was beginning to face stiff competition from trams and buses. Plans to electrify the line and make it part of the underground system came to nothing and the last passenger train ran on 3 July 1954, with the line being closed completely in 1970.

After the footbridge over the main line, the walk takes on a more rural character. There are few mature trees, except those close to the boundary fences, well away from the track bed. This is the result

THE WALK

a well-defined gravel path to a footbridge over some railway tracks, then cross it.

▶ **2** Turn to follow a clear path alongside the railway line. Continue for 2 miles (3km), passing Stroud Green Station ⓐ and Crouch Hill Station ⓑ.

▶ **3** About 50 yards (45m) before the twin tunnels ⓒ, veer left up the bank along the path signposted 'Holmesdale Road'. Turn right, and then right again at Archway Road, passing The Shepherds pub. Turn right along Shepherds Hill and cross the road.

Gardens, continue for 250 yards (230m), then as the road starts to rise look for an opening on the left.

▶ **6** Follow the path, indicated by an old, cast-iron, green-painted signpost, to the bottom of the dip and another green signpost. Bear left up the hill and continue for 100 yards (90m).

▶ **7** At a road, cross over and pick up the path on the other side. Continue past another green signpost near a pavilion ⓓ. Turn left and walk up the hill to Muswell Hill Road.

FINSBURY PARK – ALEXANDRA PALACE

This linear walk starts from Finsbury Park Underground Station. Catch a bus to return from Alexandra Palace.

▶ **1** Turn left out of the station into Station Place, cross over Stroud Green Road and look for the entrance to Finsbury Park in a high brick wall before the railway bridge. Ascend the snaking path and follow

▶ **4** After 40 yards (35m) turn left before the half-timbered library down a track marked by a concrete bollard. Walk downhill, ignoring a path to the right.

▶ **5** Turn right at Priory

of railway companies mowing the banks, as well as frequent grass fires caused by sparks from passing steam locomotives. Only in recent years has the vegetation been allowed to grow. The habitat therefore resembles that found in a young deciduous wood.

BUTTERFLIES

The walk opens out as the track follows a slight embankment. The grassy banks are particularly good for butterflies; you may see meadow browns, small coppers, large skippers, or even the bright, day-flying six-spot burnet moth.

Further on, by the bridge over

Stapleton Hall Road, is the white painted Station House of what was once Stroud Green Station ⓐ. Until recently it was used as a wildlife centre for the Parkland Walk, but lack of funds has forced its closure.

THROUGH THE STATION

After a bridge decorated with a mural, the grassy mound of Crouch Hill's covered reservoir comes into view on the right. A little further along the route there is a well equipped adventure playground.

After going under a footbridge, you arrive at the remains of Crouch Hill Station ⓑ, where there are platforms on each side of the old track

▲*The old iron railway bridge near Crouch End has been enlivened with murals painted by local children.*

8 Go over the pedestrian crossing and enter Highgate Wood through New Gate. Turn immediately right up a clearly defined path. When you reach a private aviary at the back of a house in the wood, head left along the path that leads towards a group of buildings, which are a café and toilets.

9 Walk along the path leading away from the back of the café. When you come to a drinking fountain, the path splits. Turn left along the main path.

10 Keeping inside the wood, turn right along a path parallel to its edge. Leave the wood and turn left along a road. Pass under a road bridge and turn right along Parkland Walk, the old railway bed. Continue past a fine viewpoint **E** until the path ends at Muswell Hill. Head through a pedestrian tunnel under the road and turn right.

11 Go along a covered walkway to The Grove, part of Alexandra Park. Take the left fork in the tarmac path to an open area by a café. Walk through the park, past the car park, then cross a road to reach Alexandra Palace **F**.

attracts butterflies. A little further on, this section of the Parkland Walk ends at the point where the old line plunged into twin tunnels **C** beneath Highgate Hill.

Queen's Wood, with its mature trees, is a very attractive green oasis in a heavily built-up area. Within it stands a pavilion **D** with a clock tower. Beneath its verandah is a granite slab set into the wall, recording that it was royally designated as an open space in 1898.

Next you come to the 70-acre (28-hectare) Highgate Wood. It was

▼*As you walk through the shaded cutting at Crouch Hill you will see an overgrown viaduct. The route then passes along the attractive, leafy paths of Queen's Wood (left) in Highgate.*

◀*In Highgate Wood an old marble drinking fountain stands refreshingly at a junction of tarmac paths.*

bed. The next section is overgrown and in a cutting; it can be cool here, even on a hot day. Great hairy willowherb grows here, enjoying the moist, shady conditions. Ivy covers the ground and the trees.

As you approach Highgate, elegant homes with well-cared-for back gardens can occasionally be glimpsed to either side of the track. After the track crosses over Northwood Road, it is again quite overgrown; at the end of summer, a profusion of buddleia bushes

originally a part of the old Forest of Middlesex and was donated to the Corporation of London in 1885. The wood is a wildlife haven. About 70 species of birds have been recorded here, including such rarities as golden orioles and buzzards, but treecreepers and woodpeckers are more common. The wood's mammals include foxes, woodmice and rabbits, as well as the ubiquitous grey squirrels. Attempts are being made to encourage bats, with some success, as three different species have been recorded.

A Roman pottery was excavated in the northern end of the wood after an archaeologist spotted

ALL PHOTOS: DAVID HUGHES

broken shards on the ground in 1962; the finds are now in the Museum of London. The pottery, which operated intermittently from about 43 BC to the beginning of the 2nd century AD, probably supplied Londinium down the hill.

You pick up the railway line again after leaving Highgate Wood at its northernmost end. The bridge over St James's Lane provides a good view to Muswell Hill, with its attractive architecture, quiet streets and Victorian church.

▶*As you rejoin the old line after Highgate Wood the Parkland Walk follows a good path to Muswell Hill.*

ALL PHOTOS: DAVID HUGHES

The People's Palace

Alexandra Palace was never a royal residence. It was opened on 24 May 1873 as a 'People's Palace', a north London rival to Sydenham's Crystal Palace in the south. The original glass and steel buildings burned down just 16 days later, after having been visited by over 124,000 people.

It was rebuilt and reopened on 1 May 1875. The building centred on the Great Hall, which could seat up to 14,000. Other parts of the palace housed displays of paintings and sculptures, exhibitions, a museum, lecture hall and library, banqueting rooms, a 3,500-seater concert room (subsequently turned into a roller skating rink) and a 3,000-seater theatre.

In the grounds were a race track — known affectionately to those who live around these parts as 'The Frying Pan' — a trotting ring, a cricket ground, ornamental lakes and a permanent fun-fair. It was massively popular up to the turn of the century when, after financial difficulties, the complex became the responsibility of the local authorities who were required to make it 'available for the free use and recreation of the public forever'.

In 1934, the palace found new fame when part of the building was leased to the BBC for its pioneering TV broadcasts. Programmes were produced there for almost 20 years, and the Corporation's broadcasting mast became a familiar landmark on the London skyline.

On 10 July 1980, another disastrous fire destroyed the Great Hall, banqueting suite and roller rink, together with the dressing rooms belonging to the main theatre. Although it was decided to rebuild at once, some sections have not yet been finished.

The dramatic architecture of Alexandra Palace, with its arches, balconies and rose window, does justice to its fine position.

▼*The viaduct from St James's Lane provides fine views over Muswell Hill and of east and south-east London.*

At about this point, the old railway viaduct ❸ gives you an unexpected and spectacular view of east and south-east London, dominated by the distant Canary Wharf Tower, capped with a pyramid, as well as the unmistakable outline of the Isle of Dogs. In the middle distance are the green islands of Finsbury Park and Clissold Park. As you walk along the viaduct, you can see further south, with the NatWest Tower poking up over a low ridge.

ACROSS THE PARK

At Muswell Hill, you leave the old railway, but it is now only a short, pleasant walk through The Grove — part of Alexandra Park — to the magnificent buildings of Alexandra Palace itself ❻. The park here is worth exploring too, and boasts some good leisure facilities.

◀Surrounded by its enormous moat, Bodiam Castle was calculated to daunt any invader. The pygmy shrew (above), Britain's smallest mammal, can be found in grassland on the walk.

A well preserved castle overlooking a tranquil river valley

Few castles look as impressive or impregnable as Bodiam. The massive circular towers gave a wide field of fire for bowmen and primitive artillery, while the wide, deep moat eliminated the possibility of undermining, a favourite tactic of besieging medieval armies.

Bodiam Castle Ⓐ was built by Sir Edward Dalyngrigge. It was completed in 1388 and represented the distilled experience of 300 years of castle building. A bridge over the moat led to an octagonal island fortification. From there, it was necessary to make a right-angled turn and cross a drawbridge to a fortified tower. Only after crossing yet another drawbridge and negotiating three pairs of gates and three portcullises (one still survives), could entry be made.

EFFECTIVE DETERRENT

Bodiam was built in response to raids by the French during the 100 Years War, when Winchelsea and Rye were both sacked. At this time, the River Rother was navigable, and the castle thus guarded a possible

invasion route to London from the south. It was never put to the test, however. The fortification did witness a skirmish in the Wars of the Roses, and was partially dismantled by Parliamentarians in the Civil War to stop it being used by Royalists.

The walk begins by rounding three sides of the moat, giving a good view of the formidable defence. A lane passes the re-sited bridge and runs uphill to a road.

FACT FILE

- ☀ Bodiam, 12 miles (19.2km) east of Heathfield, on the B2165

- Pathfinder 1270 (TQ 62/72), grid reference TQ 785254

  miles 0 1 2 3 4 5 6 7 8 9 10 miles
  kms 0 1 2 3 4 5 6 7 8 9 10 11 12 13 14 15 kms

- ◔ Allow 2½ hours

- ▬ One fairly steep climb. Good paths and lanes throughout. May be muddy in wet weather

- P Car park at the start

- ⅋ Two tea-rooms and a pub that serves food in Bodiam

- ⌂ Bodiam Castle is open daily, 10am-6pm or sunset if earlier. Free to members of the National Trust

Opposite is a tall, Gothic schoolhouse Ⓑ with a conspicuous, wooden clock tower painted white.

A quiet path runs downhill to the village and affords wide views over the valley ahead. Beyond the Castle Inn, the route follows the bank of the Rother Ⓒ. The river is still navigable for small craft as far as Bodiam Bridge, and a boat service runs in summer from Northiam. However, as you head upstream the river becomes too narrow, and reeds and water-lilies grow in abundance. In summer, the pink and mauve blossoms of comfrey grow in profusion on the banks. The herb is still occasionally used as a poultice for sprains and bruises.

Soon after passing a new pumping station, the route joins a road to

▼Bodiam's old schoolhouse, a Victorian Gothic building, has an elegant wooden clock tower.

THE WALK

BODIAM – SNAGSHALL

The walk begins in the National Trust car park by Bodiam Castle Ⓐ.

1 Follow the path to the castle and walk anti-clockwise around three sides of the moat to the ticket office. Follow the lane uphill and around a bend to a road, opposite the old schoolhouse Ⓑ. Turn left. After a few paces, take the path on your right, which runs downhill, parallel to the road, past the Castle Inn to a bridge across the River Rother Ⓒ. Just before the bridge, take the path on your right along the bank of the river and follow it for a mile (1.6km), until you reach a road.

2 Turn left and cross a bridge. After 50 yards (45m), turn left on the drive to Udiam Farmhouse. After a few paces, cross two stiles on your right and go diagonally left uphill through a field. At the top, pass through a gate and turn right along a track. After passing through a gate into an orchard, bear left, following a bridlepath uphill to a small water

tower. Continue ahead through a gate and immediately bear right into a field. Cross to a path in the far corner, into a wood. In a few paces, turn left on a crossing track through the trees. Follow it for just over ¼ mile (400m) until you reach a road.

3 Cross to the road opposite, signposted to Ewhurst Green. Pass a high sandstone embankment Ⓓ and follow this road for almost ½ mile (800m) to Old Shoreham House.

Follow the road around a sharp bend and downhill. After about 200 yards (180m), fork right. At the drive to Romery Lodge, turn left to head downhill, with a wooden fence on your right, to a stile into a field. Continue to the bottom of the field to an opening, marked by a signpost, in the wire fence on your left. Turn right through the opening and walk towards a tree-lined hedge. Cross a wooden hurdle and ditch into a

field. Keep to the left and walk towards a tall barn left of a line of poplars. Go left round the barn and cross over the disused railway track Ⓔ.

4 Turn right in the field beyond the railway and go round two sides of it to the flood embankment. Turn left towards Bodiam Bridge. Just before the bridge, bear left to a gate into a road. Turn right and go over the bridge to return to the car park.

---

cross the river. On the other side, a new path leads around an attractive, tile-hung farmhouse at Udiam.

A bridleway and an old boundary lane lead you to a natural embankment of sandstone Ⓓ, some 8 feet (2.4m) high. Down the hill to the north is the aptly named Rocks Farm, and, a little further on, a disused quarry. It was from local stone such as this, probably cut here, that much of Bodiam Castle was built.

FULL STEAM AHEAD

At Ewhurst Green, the route heads north to an overgrown railway track Ⓔ. This was the Kent and East Sussex line, which ran from

▼*The dovecotes attached to the wall of this stone barn at Udiam are home to a delightful flock of white doves.*

JASON SMALLEY

Robertsbridge to Tenterden. Enthusiasts are gradually restoring the line, which closed to passenger traffic in 1954 and freight in 1961. Steam trains currently run from Tenterden to Northiam, and are expected to continue to Bodiam by 1998.

From the railway, there is an impressive view of the castle across the flat fields. On the south-facing slopes behind it are rows of grape vines, which thrive on the sandy soil and produce increasingly popular Sussex wines. On the other side of the field is the Rother, high-banked to prevent flooding. The walk follows this embankment to return to Bodiam and the car park.

HORSES AND COURSES

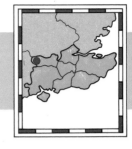

ROB SCOTT. INSET: GDT-SILVESTRIS/NHPA

A walk on open downland and along a disused railway

Lambourn Valley is racehorse country. There are racing stables down in the valley and gallops where the horses are exercised and trained on the hills above.

The walk begins in the charming village of East Garston Ⓐ. It is spread out along the River Lambourn, which in dry weather is no more than a trickle and sometimes even disappears altogether. The older village houses reflect the fact that good building stone is virtually nonexistent in this area. Almost all the cottages are timber-framed, but a rich variety of materials has been used to fill in the walls. Brick is a common material. Sometimes light-coloured 'headers' — bricks laid at right angles to the face of the wall so that only their

'heads' show — alternate with darker 'stretchers' to create a chequered effect, known as diaper work. Interesting effects are also created by using knobbly flints for walls and there is a particularly attractive use of tiles on a gable end at Church

---

FACT FILE

- East Garston, 3 miles (5 km) south-east of Lambourn
- Pathfinders 1154 (SU 28/38) and 1170 (SU 27/37), grid reference SU 362768

miles 0	1	2	3	4	5	6	7	8	9	10 miles

kms 0	1	2	3	4	5	6	7	8	9	10	11	12	13	14	15 kms

- Allow 3 hours
- Steep in places and some paths are muddy when wet
- P East Garston village
- Public house and shop at East Garston and Eastbury

▲ *The Lambourn Valley has a racing tradition, but in East Garston some people ride just for the pleasure of it. On the surrounding downs, hares (inset) can be found 'boxing' in spring.*

Cottage, near the beginning of the walk. Thatch is widely used for roofing, sometimes sweeping in attractive curves round tiny first-floor windows: there is even a house that boasts a thatched garage. One very attractive feature is the use of little footbridges across the river to link cottages on the south bank.

FARMYARD

The road swings round towards the church and ends in a broad track that runs through the farmyard of Manor Farm. On the right is a group of stables, but although these are the first to be met along the walk, it is unlikely that you will have come this far without at least a glimpse of a horse. The village street regularly echoes to the rhythmic clip-clop of

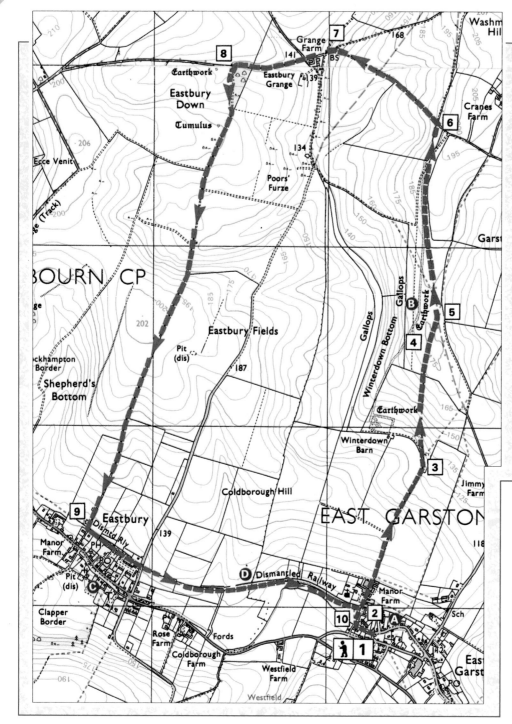

EAST GARSTON – EASTBURY

The walk starts by the post office in the village of East Garston Ⓐ.

1 Cross the bridge over the river and turn left. Continue following the road as it turns round to the right past Downlands.

2 At Manor Farm continue straight on through the farmyard.

3 Where the broad track swings round to the left, continue straight on uphill in the direction indicated by the footpath sign. Take great care as the footpath may have been planted over and may not be easy to follow.

4 At the top of the hill cross the fence. This brings

▲*Local building materials are rare. Houses in Eastbury and East Garston are mostly timber-framed and brick.*

hooves as the strings of racehorses head to and from the downs.

Once past the farm, the special nature of the downland becomes apparent. The Downs were once part of a great dome of chalk that stretched not just across southern England but all the way to France. During the millions of years of geological time, the sea broke through to create the English Channel and rivers formed valleys that split up the downs into separate regions. Over the centuries, the soft chalk weathered, gently and slowly eroding to create the smooth curves, the

dips and hollows and the rounded hills that are such a feature of the region. This is a very open landscape, of wide vistas, but it is by no means an empty landscape.

At first the track runs through farmland. The soil is thin but modern agriculture with its artificial fertilizers has made it possible to grow crops on it. The nature of that soil is particularly evident in winter, when it has a curious whitish tinge, created by the chalk and the flint nodules that can be seen scattered over the ground. The path climbs gently uphill, then dips down

towards Winterdown Bottom. The barn at the foot of the hill is home to a surprising occupant — not livestock, nor fodder, but a light aircraft.

Then the path climbs steeply over the last of the farmland to reach the grassland of the ridge that marks the high point of East Garston Down Ⓑ. Here are the gallops, marked out by a row of neat, numbered white posts which not only mark out the course but are used by trainers for timing you into an area set out with steeplechase jumps **B**. Leave the jumps on your left and head for the stile.

5 ▶ At the stile turn left to follow the line of the fence.

6 ▶ Cross further stile. At the broad track, turn left.

7 ▶ At the farm, continue straight on, leaving farm buildings on your left, along the track marked 'By Way'.

8 ▶ At the far side of the copse, turn left onto the broad track with the copse on your left, then a group of conifers on your left.

Continue straight ahead for about 1½ miles (2.5 km).

9 ▶ At the edge of the village of Eastbury **C**, turn left to cross the stile by the footpath sign. Past the first house, go through the gate and turn right by the wire fence, cross the stile and

turn left. The path crosses a series of stiles and appears to go through gardens before joining the obvious track of the disused railway **D**.

10 ▶ Beyond the church, turn right to rejoin the road to return to the start.

the horses. Here too are practice fences. If you have never seen a steeplechase fence at close quarters, you may be surprised at both the height and depth of these daunting obstacles. It is obviously essential that walkers keep well clear of horses being put through their paces.

Horses do not have the downs to themselves. In spring, in particular,

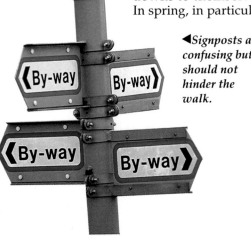

◀ *Signposts are confusing but should not hinder the walk.*

this is a good place for watching hares, which can sometimes be seen up on their hind legs 'boxing' with each other, and rabbits are even more common. The skylark is a popular resident, rising above the nesting ground with its clear warbling song. Where the skylark seems a solitary bird, the lapwing is altogether more gregarious and flocks of the birds, flashing their black and white plumage in the sun, add their 'peewit' cry to the downland air.

SPLENDID VIEWS

The path continues over the grassland, rising now altogether more gently as it goes. It is worth pausing occasionally to look back at the splendid views over the Lambourn Valley. At the top of the hill, the walk returns to farmland where in

▼ *The rolling open hills of the Berkshire Downs provide the perfect countryside to train racehorses.*

winter and early spring the furrows of the plough accentuate the curves of the hills. The farm track leads on down to the farm of Eastbury Grange. The house itself sits comfortably in a little hollow, given extra shelter by a screen of trees, while the farm buildings are spread out around it. Just beyond the farm is a small copse, a narrow finger of

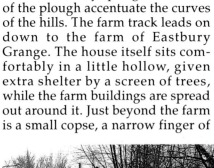

▲ *You would be very unlucky to make it right round the walk without seeing at least one horse.*

trees that points away south down the hillside. It seems a meagre covering of woodland, but it is enough to provide a home for the local deer population. Sometimes, they are surprised by walkers and go dashing off across the fields showing their distinctive white rumps.

VILLAGES

The broad track dips then rises steeply to the high point of the downs before descending steadily to the village of Eastbury **C**. Eastbury itself is, not surprisingly, similar in character to neighbouring East Garston. Again, it is based on a main village street running along the

The History of Horse Racing

Horse racing goes back to antiquity — at least as far as the chariot races of Greece and Rome — but racing as we know it in Britain dates back to the Stuart kings. It was James I who established stables at Newmarket where he kept racehorses and 'riders for the races' — the first royal jockeys. By the end of the 17th century racecourses had spread around the country, and breeders began introducing Arabian stock. Three of these stallions were

stables were established for training the horses. Suitable regions needed to have extensive areas of open grassland over which gallops could be laid for practice. The Berkshire Downs proved ideal for the purpose. The flinty, chalky soil was considered too poor for ploughing, but once the trees had been cleared it developed as springy turf, used for grazing. Stables were developed in the villages of the Lambourn Valley and each day horses are led up to

▲ *Steeplechasing is also practised on the Downs. The size of the fences appears daunting to the walker.*

a former railway **D**, as becomes abundantly clear once you are quite clear of the houses.

The Lambourn Valley Railway was begun in 1898 under the Light Railway Act. This allowed for railways being built on the cheap, to lower standards than those that applied to their bigger brethren.

SAFETY FACTORS

Safety factors were less stringently applied, but there was a price to be paid in slower trains and poorer service. Thanks to the Act, however, many regions were served by railways which would otherwise have been denied them, and the little Lambourn Valley Railway was, for a time, a real boon to the horse-racing community. It could not, however, compete with the motor car and the horse box. Sadly, the line closed in 1960. Much of the character of the line is, however, still clear.

The rolling chalk downlands of Berkshire make the perfect exercise and training ground for racehorses.

the sires from which all 'thoroughbreds' are descended.

Racing developed as a sport in two broad categories: flat racing and racing over jumps — either the high fences of the steeplechase or the less demanding hurdles. Special

gallops such as those of Winterdown for exercise and training over the jumps.

So-called modern training methods were introduced in the 1840s. Before that horses were taken on long gallops, swathed in heavy rugs to make them sweat. Today's trainers are more scientific, choosing the training methods best suited to each individual horse.

River Lambourn, and again the older houses and cottages are timber-framed with thatched roofs. Some of the larger barns have now been converted into private houses. The walk itself runs rather curiously, through the gardens of houses, but it is nevertheless a public right-of-way. Walkers, however, must be sure to follow the signs and cross fences by the stiles. Near the beginning, the path passes a field on the left, and it is worth pausing to look at the iron gateposts. These are a distinctive shape in cross-section – Ω – and they

were originally railway track. They were used on the old Great Western Railway in the days when it was broad gauge, with rails set 7 feet (2.1 metres) apart instead of the standard 4 ft 8½ ins (1.4 metres) in use on the rest of the system and used throughout Britain today. You can also see an old goods wagon in use as a store in the fields. In fact this footpath is following the line of

▶ *It is traditional for racing stables to have a weather vane in the shape of a horse. This is a splendid variation.*

Along the Dorset Coast Path to an old smugglers' haunt

Chalk cliffs leading down to secluded bays make this part of the Dorset coastline particularly attractive. Inland, there are small villages to explore and the Dorset Coast Path gives walkers excellent views in good weather. The high spot of the walk undoubtedly occurs just past Osmington Mills **B**, when the path suddenly bursts upon the cliff top and there is a view over a great expanse of sea to Weymouth.

The route covers an area northeast of Weymouth, where the scenery is very diverse due to differences in the underlying rocks. These change from Purbeck stone to Kimmeridge clay, to Corallian limestone then to chalk. The rocks of the

FACT FILE

- ☀ Osmington, 5 miles (8 km) south-east of Dorchester

- ▣ Pathfinder 1332 (SY 68/78), grid reference SY 724830

  miles 0 1 2 3 4 5 6 7 8 9 10 miles
  kms 0 1 2 3 4 5 6 7 8 9 10 11 12 13 14 15 kms

- ◔ Allow 3 hours

- ▬ Wet grass may be encountered near the start of the walk. Muddy at Lower Dairy Farm after wet weather

- Ⓟ In Osmington

- Ⓣ Bus service from Weymouth

- ▥ The Sunray at Osmington. Tearoom overlooking the sea
- 🍴 and the Smugglers' Inn at Osmington Mills

- ⓦⓒ At Osmington Mills

▲Smugglers' Inn at Osmington Mills is a reminder of the illegal dealings that once took place here. The Mother Shipton moth (inset) flies during the day.

heathland area, the Bagshot Beds, are never far away.

Osmington **A** is a village of thatched stone cottages and stone garden walls. The cottages are adorned with flowers and valerian grows outwards from the walls. One of the cottages has a thatched roof embellished with crescent-shaped decorations called scallops.

Adjoining the churchyard are the ruins of the 17th-century manor house, where steps lead down to a very old door with long iron hinges.

PETER BAKER/PHOTOBANK INTERNATIONAL. INSET: PAUL STERRY/NATURE PHOTOGRAPHERS LTD

THE WALK

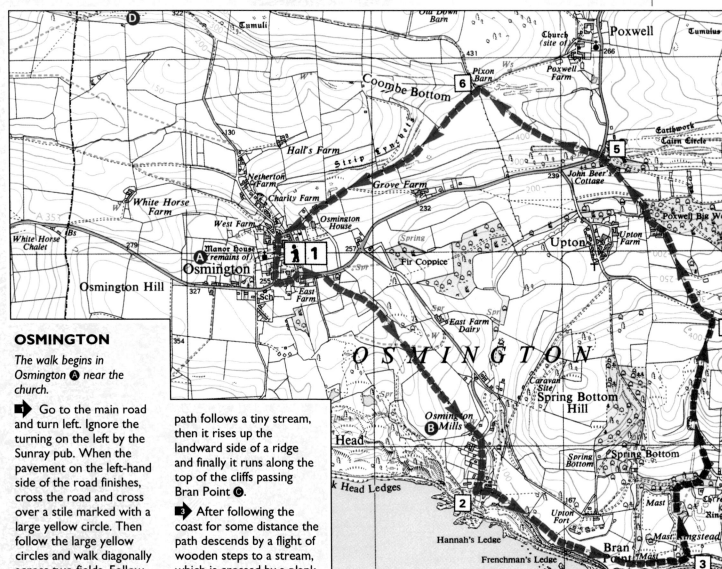

OSMINGTON

The walk begins in Osmington Ⓐ near the church.

▶1 Go to the main road and turn left. Ignore the turning on the left by the Sunray pub. When the pavement on the left-hand side of the road finishes, cross the road and cross over a stile marked with a large yellow circle. Then follow the large yellow circles and walk diagonally across two fields. Follow the path across the third field and continue in the same direction along the right-hand side of a hedge until you come to a stile. Go over the stile and continue along a shady path. When you come to a road, turn right to the seaside hamlet of Osmington Mills Ⓑ.

▶2 At the end of the road turn left at the signpost. Cross Upton Brook (which is crossed here by no fewer than six wooden bridges), turn left at the entrance to Smugglers' Inn, then turn right along the side of the inn. At first the

path follows a tiny stream, then it rises up the landward side of a ridge and finally it runs along the top of the cliffs passing Bran Point Ⓒ.

▶3 After following the coast for some distance the path descends by a flight of wooden steps to a stream, which is crossed by a plank bridge. Turn left and follow the stream through a wood until you come to a concrete bridge. Go over the bridge and ascend the left bank of a smaller stream. The path bends right over the tributary and continues through the wood. When you come to a lane go straight on. The lane bends right and then left and comes to a junction. Bear right here, and keep straight on until you come to a road.

▶4 Turn left and follow the road up a little valley to a T-junction. Turn left again and after about 70 yards

(63 metres) go through a farm gate on the right, down a track towards some farm buildings. Keep to the track and onto a road which leads up a gentle slope to the main road, the A353.

▶5 Cross the main road with care, go through a farm gate and up a track on the right-hand side of a small valley. When the track fades, aim for a solitary hawthorn bush leaning to the right and continue in the same direction until the grey

slate roof of Pixon Barn comes into view.

▶6 At the unmetalled road, bear left through two gates (one before and one after Pixon Barn). The Osmington White Horse Ⓓ is to your right. Keep going in the same direction, following first a fence and then a stone wall. Continue through a farm gate and down a shady track to a road in the village of Osmington. Go straight ahead for 80 yards (72 metres), then turn left to return to the start.

▶ *While staying in Osmington in 1861, Constable painted* Weymouth Bay. *The painting hangs in the National Gallery.*

NATIONAL GALLERY, LONDON

Nature Walk

THE NIGHTJAR winters in Africa, but flies to Britain towards the end of April. It seeks out lowland heath and chalk downland, typical of the landscape surrounding Osmington.

THE NIGHTJAR is difficult to spot as it is most active at night and is well camouflaged by its colouring. In flight, white tail and wing patches show as it swoops while hunting its insect prey.

THE BIRD has a huge mouth. If other birds attempt to invade the nest, it threatens them by hissing. It scoops up insects with its wide gape, which is surrounded by bristles.

CHRIS ROSE

In 1816, the artist John Constable spent his honeymoon in the village. He produced two paintings of the area, one entitled *Osmington Village* and the other *Weymouth Bay.*

From Osmington Mills the route follows part of the Dorset Coast Path, which takes to the hills here to avoid the built-up area around Weymouth. From this height there is a beautiful view to the left looking along a valley to Holworth. The Osmington White Horse ❶ can be clearly seen from here. This is the only white horse chalk figure that has a rider — King George III, who was a regular visitor to this part of the country. There is a view of the Osmington White Horse towards the end of the walk, just past Pixon Barn. From here it is possible to see the chalk figure on the right of the chalk escarpment.

CLIFF-TOP INN

The Smugglers' Inn at Osmington Mills is described on the signboard as a 13th-century smugglers' haunt, but the present building is not as old as this. There used to be a cliff-top path to the west from here, but from the far end of the car park it is clear how this path has now completely disappeared as a result of erosion by the sea. This evidence of erosion makes it possible to imagine Britain becoming separated from France

▶ *A section of the walk follows the Dorset Coast Path. The headland of White Nothe can be seen to the east.*

and the Isle of Wight from the mainland, over thousands of years.

Before long the path passes through a thicket; when it emerges the headland of White Nothe comes into view ahead, with St Adhelm's Head to the right of it. In the novel *Moonfleet* by J Meade Falkner, John Trenchard was carried up the cliff path to White Nothe by Elzevir Block. Along the shore there is a wreck of an old ship whose bare ribs are a favourite perch for cormorants. At Bran Point ❻ there is a series of ledges of Corallian limestone which dip away to the east.

WOODLAND GREENERY

The path passes a meadow where bird's-foot trefoil grows, then it descends into a little valley. Here the route turns into a wood, where hart's tongue fern and pendulous sedge flourish. Hart's tongue does not look like a fern as its leaves are not divided up into pinnae (feathery

PETER BAKER/PHOTOBANK INTERNATIONAL

71

fronds). However, you can identify it as a fern by the fruiting bodies on the back of the leaves. Pendulous sedge may be recognized as a sedge by its triangular stems.

CHALK QUARRY

On leaving the wood, the route follows a lane through lush meadows backed by woodland. Another stretch of woodland comes later on the route, but the vegetation is not as luxuriant here as it is in the valley.

A wide variety of wild flowers grows in the valley, but pride of place must go to the nodding thistles with their big, round purple flower-heads. On the left is a quarry where the chalk may be seen dipping to the north. The chalk was formed over a period of 30 million years from the skeletons of tiny animals called diatoms that accumulated on the floor of the sea.

Along the right-hand side of the valley there are traces of ancient cultivation terraces called strip lynchets. Both sides of the valley are covered in gorse bushes, which attract stonechats.

From the top of the hill, a Bronze Age burial mound (or tumulus) can be seen in a field on the left. There are 1,800 of these tumuli in Dorset.

LARK SONG

The final section of the walk passes Pixon Barn, which is an isolated stone building with a slate roof and walled farmyard. Rabbits are common in this area, and larks may be heard singing overhead. As the route descends, it runs along the crest of a ridge with views on both sides. On the left, the Isle of Portland is linked to the mainland

The Smugglers' Route

Between about 1750 and 1840 vast quantities of smuggled brandy, tea, silk and tobacco were brought ashore on the south coast of England and distributed inland by wagon or packhorse. One of the regular landing places was Osmington Mills and from 1790 until 1800 what is now Smugglers' Inn was the headquarters of the smuggler-chief Pierre la Tour, who was known in England as French Peter. He eventually married the landlord's daughter, Arabella Carless, and took her back to France with him, where they lived comfortably on his illicit fortune. It was not until much later that the inn acquired its present name.

The smugglers' route from Osmington Mills to Sherborne passed the cottage at Lower Bockhampton where Thomas Hardy was born in 1840. Smuggling had ceased by Hardy's time, but it obviously caught the boy's imagination. He remembered his grandfather telling him how he had hidden kegs of smuggled spirit in the cottage and cut a window in the side of the porch to look out for Revenue Officers. The cottage was ideally situated as a staging post as it was on the edge of the heath.

Wreckers tried to cause shipwrecks deliberately, to profit from the cargo.

The route used by the smugglers, called Snail Creep, can still be seen to this day running north and south from the cottage.

by no more than a narrow strip of shingle; on the right is a valley of Kimmeridge clay and you can see the village of Sutton Poyntz. The white horse is also visible, but it appears to be foreshortened because of the angle. Finally, the route follows a lane shaded by sycamore trees, which leads back into Osmington. A giant ammonite can be seen in a house wall — a common sight in this fossiliferous county.

▶ *The Osmington White Horse was produced, like other hill figures, by cutting the turf away from a chalk hillside. If not regularly weeded, vegetation grows back, obscuring the figure. The roofs of Poxwell Manor (above left) in Poxwell village.*

THE AVON NAVIGATION

ROB SCOTT

brought a vast amount of new boating activity to the river, as can be seen from the bustling marina by the bridge. The waterway was not, however, built with pleasure boating in mind. Two centuries ago, Keynsham was the centre of a thriving brass industry. Avon mill, upstream from the bridge and dignified by a little cupola, was once used for brass-working. The mill featured no fewer than eight water wheels to run the appropriate machinery.

◀ *A late-afternoon view along the Avon just west of Bath — once a busy waterway, it is now devoted to leisure uses. Each spike of the tufted vetch (below) can carry up to 30 flowers.*

G. J. CAMBRIDGE/NHPA

A walk along a towpath and an embankment that ends in Bath

This walk follows the towpath of the Avon navigation and the disused railway between Bitton and Bath, with a visit to a preserved railway. The return can be made on one of the regular trains that run from Bath to Keynsham.

Since the walk is linear it can be followed in the reverse direction. Those arriving by car will, however, find it much easier to park in Keynsham than in Bath.

ACROSS THE AVON

From Keynsham the walk begins with a short stroll down the road to the bridge across the Avon. At this point the river divides: to one side the water thunders over a weir, while to the other it passes down an artificial cutting ❶ in which a lock allows boats to pass easily up and

down. The building of the locks to make the Avon navigable between Bristol and Bath was completed in 1723. Now, however, the Avon navigation is part of an even longer waterway system, joined by the Kennet and Avon Canal to the River Thames at Reading.

Some years ago, most of the canal was derelict, but in 1990 it was reopened throughout. This has

▶ *Water pours through a pair of lock gates on the River Avon as they open to allow a boat to proceed upstream.*

ROB SCOTT

FACT FILE

✳ Keynsham

▭ Pathfinder 1183 (ST66/76), grid reference ST 656689

miles 0   1   2   3   4   5   6   7   8   9   10 miles
kms 0 1 2 3 4 5 6 7 8 9 10 11 12 13 14 15 kms

◔ Allow 4 hours

▬ Easy going on good paths

🅿 Station car park at Keynsham. If this is full there is a car park beside the first bridge on the route

🍴 Full range of facilities at Keynsham and Bath. Pub beside the walk at Saltford

THE WALK

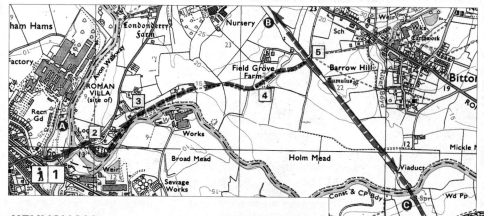

KEYNSHAM – CENTRAL BATH

The walk begins at Keynsham station and ends at Bath station.

1 From Keynsham station turn right to follow the main road downhill. Cross the main stream of the river and the lock cutting **A**.

2 Turn right by the car park and follow the signs marked 'Avon Walkway' down to the river bank. Follow the towpath beside the river, signposted to Swineford.

3 Where the towpath meets the broad track, turn left and follow the latter towards the large, square house. At the house, leave the broad track for the footpath, which continues straight on, following the line of the telegraph poles. It continues across the fields via a series of stiles.

4 Cross the stile on the left by the farm buildings and continue in the direction indicated by the yellow arrow here. At the broad track leading up to the farm, turn diagonally to the right, past a stone barn. Continue on the path via more stiles, heading towards the prominent railway bridge.

5 At the bridge, take the path up the right-hand side of the arch to reach the top of the embankment. Turn left to visit the steam railway **B**, about 1,100 yards (1 km) along the embankment. Then return to this point and continue towards Bath. The route continues straight on along the old railway, over the first of the river viaducts **C** and past the village of Saltford **D**.

6 Immediately beyond the bridge across the river on the outskirts of Bath, turn right past the drinking fountain to the towpath. Continue in the same direction along the towpath to the heart of the city **E**.

7 The towpath ends at Broad Quay. Continue straight on down Dorchester Street to the station for trains back to Keynsham.

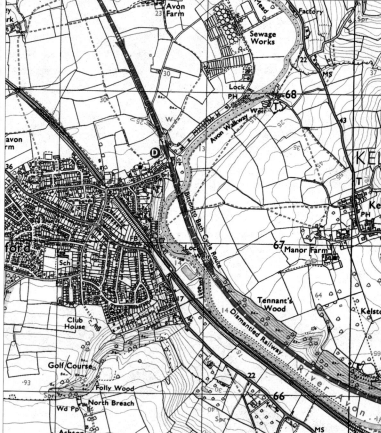

A more likely-looking candidate for heavy industry can be seen downstream, where the view is dominated by a bulky red-brick factory with a tall chimney. It is not, however, brass they make here, but chocolate. The factory is, in fact, part of the Cadbury empire.

The walk briefly follows the tow-path of the River Avon — a

The church tower in Bitton village, which can be seen from the vantage-point of the railway embankment.

reminder that in the early working days of the navigation, boats were pulled by horses. Soon, however, the path strikes off across the fields. To the right, across the river, you can see the present main railway line from Bristol to Bath, while up ahead is the high embankment of the disused railway, the next stage of the walk. A high-arched bridge carries the former line, and it is here that walkers join the railway route.

After the line's closure in 1971, a local organization was set up with the aim of converting the track-bed into a safe inter-city route for cyclists and walkers. The scheme has proved a great success — there are similar schemes in other areas.

But there are still trains to be seen at the old Bitton station. By turning left on the embankment, you come to the track **B**, where steam and diesel locomotives are to be seen at work on open days.

THE HIGH GROUND

Returning to the bridge and continuing towards Bath, you soon discover one of the advantages of walking old railways: the embankment provides an airy viewpoint for seeing the surrounding countryside. To the right, you look across the flat fields to the river, while to the left is the village of Bitton, with its prominent church tower and the hills rising behind it. Between the bank and the village is a rounded, grassy hump, a prehistoric burial site or round barrow, still remembered by the name Barrow Hill.

The approach to the river is marked by lines of pollarded willows along the hedgerows. Once across the first of the river viaducts **C** a picnic area offers the first sight of the 'sculpture trail' laid out along the walkway. Here large blocks of stone have been covered with vari-

▶ *One of the large carvings in the sculpture trail that embellishes one side of the river. The Saxon style of the sculptures alludes to a nearby Anglo-Saxon burial ground.*

ous devices: faces, a jar, a short sword, a shield and so on. The theme is Saxon, reflecting the fact that an Anglo-Saxon burial ground is sited close by.

Gradually the track cuts deeper into the ground, in a familiar pattern of railway building. The engineers dug a cutting through the rising ground, and used the spoil to build up the embankment across the valley. It creates a rather secretive, enclosed world, undisturbed except by the songs of birds.

Now, instead of the line crossing over lanes and roads, it goes beneath them, and one can see the simple, no-nonsense style of the bridges, built with stone abutments and brick arches.

A KISSING SEAT

At Saltford **D** there is easy access to the village, via steps that go down past the Bird in Hand public house. Continuing across the river, you will encounter a 'kissing seat' — another sculptured feature — with a view over boathouses and the lock. Among the buildings downstream

from the lock you can just make out a stone chimney, marking the remains of another old brass mill.

The nature of the walk changes again, now running along the side of a hill. To the right is the river, and alongside is the railway line, which

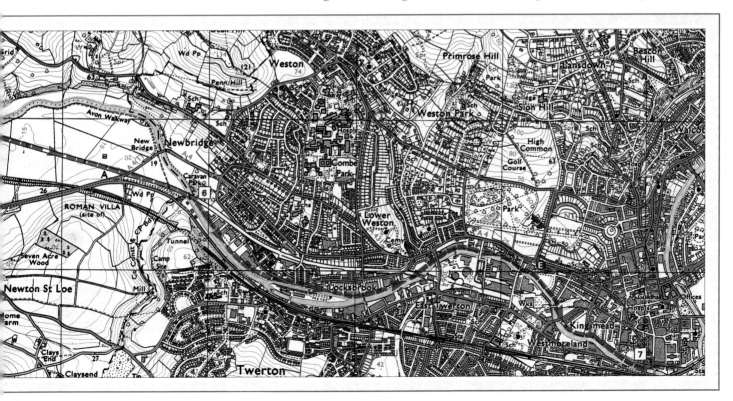

once belonged to the Great Western Railway. To the left, the hill is wooded with coppice trees, interspersed with solitary tall oaks and rows of young birch along the track. By the next bridge is another carved seat, ingeniously created from interlocking former railway sleepers.

BATH STONE

The road soon crosses the track, and it is worth looking at the underside of the 19th-century bridge to see the construction technique, with brick arches between the girders supporting the roadway. Beyond the bridge, you can look across to your left to see the 18th-century road bridge over the river. It provides the first hint of the architectural elegance for which Bath is famous. The whole structure is built from the beautiful, richly coloured Bath stone.

The next bridge marks the end of the railway section of this walk. To the right across the bridge is the last of the sculptures, a fountain that

▼ *The final part of the walk encounters this handsome bridge, its style reminiscent of the elegant buildings to be found in the heart of the city.*

A Station from the Age of Steam

Much of this walk is along the line of the former Midland Railway route from Bath to Mangotsfield on the outskirts of Bristol, where the track once joined the main line from Gloucester to Bristol. Bitton has the last surviving station along the route, a simple, single-storey building, now home to the Avon Valley preserved railway. It has retained a good deal of its old atmosphere: the original Midland Railway lamp standards still look down over the platform, with its old weighing machine, and behind the main station buildings are the former goods warehouses.

There is always a good deal to see here. Carriages still line up beside the platform, two of which belonged to the London, Midland and Scottish (Railway) before nationalization. In the sidings are an old steam crane and trucks and wagons. An old locomotive awaits reconstruction; it is of a type first designed for the Midland Railway and was also in use on the Somerset and Dorset Joint Railway, which once

linked up with this line at Bath.

The railway is seen at its best, however, on those weekends when it goes back to work. Steam locomotives, dating back to 1918, join more recent diesels to give passenger rides along a short length of track. The line has been extended since services were started up again in 1983 and the plan is once again to run trains into Bath.

Lovers of steam railways will find a veritable paradise if they visit Bitton station.

not only supplies drinking water but sends a stream coursing through the carved rock. Beyond it is the river towpath, which you will follow into the heart of the city.

The first part of this towpath walk provides a view of working Bath, rather than the tourist spa. Across the river you can see a battlemented tower — not part of some

medieval castle, but the portal of the railway tunnel. Then you come to a lock, with curious metal constructions rising alongside. These, in fact, act as flood barriers.

The river runs through an industrialized area here, and it is interesting to compare the red brick of the older works with the metal and plastic of the new. The railway

once more crosses the river, but it is now no longer part of the cycleway. Beyond it are the gasometers of the former Bath Gas Works, established in 1818.

A little suspension bridge crosses the river. It was designed by a local man, James Dredge, shortly after he had lost the competition for the construction of the Clifton Bridge in Bristol. This marks the first view of one of the splendid Bath terraces, in the centre of the city **E**.

The railway crosses the river for the last time, to the former Green Park station, now converted into a supermarket. Across the water, the river is lined by a timber wharf and a succession of old mills, now converted to offices. On your side, next to the towpath, are fashionable houses, some with ornate balconies, providing a fascinating contrast between the two sides of the river in this final stretch of the walk.

The towpath ends near the heart of the city, and you can now either go on to explore Bath or continue to the station for the return trip by mainline railway to Keynsham.

ALL PHOTOS ROB SCOTT

that once carried the Lynton and Barnstaple Railway. This beautiful line, opened in 1898, proved to be commercially unsuccessful, and was closed in 1935.

The next section of the walk follows a quiet and very attractive country lane. At first there are wide

◄ *The old green way, west of Bodley, lives up to its name. It was once a main thoroughfare for travellers and cattle drovers. Common polypody fern (inset) grows on local walls and banks.*

FACT FILE

- ✳ Parracombe, 10 miles (16 km) north-east of Barnstaple
- 🗺 Pathfinder 1214 (SS 64/74), grid reference SS 674449

miles 0	1	2	3	4	5	6	7	8	9	10 miles
kms 0 1 2 3 4 5 6 7 8 9 10 11 12 13 14 15 kms										

- ◔ Allow 2 hours
- ▬ Good paths and country lanes
- Ⓟ Small car park in Parracombe or in road near St Petrock's Church
- Ⓣ Buses from Barnstaple
- 🍴 Full range of facilities in Parracombe; tea room at Churchtown
- WC At car park

From a Georgian church along an old railway line and country lanes

The walk begins at Churchtown, as the area around St Petrock's Ⓐ, Parracombe's original parish church, is known. Outside, the church is relatively undistinguished. Inside, its astonishing Georgian interior is completely intact.

The box pews include one that was set aside for the musicians who accompanied the services. A hole was cut in the boxed end to accommodate the more extravagant sweeps of the bass viol's bow. The screen, text boards, wall monuments and even the hat pegs remain as they would have been 200 years ago.

SCALE-MODEL RAILWAY

Just below the church is Fairview, a private house built alongside the track bed of the old narrow-gauge Lynton and Barnstaple Railway. In its garden, scale models of L&BR locomotives and rolling stock run on

a section of track that reproduces some original features of the line.

The route descends an old track between high banks. This soon narrows to a path running through woodland then winding around a farmstead to Heddon House, which you approach along a fine avenue.

After a short walk along the road, the route turns off again through fields and along a low embankment

► *The simple interior of St Petrock's Church is frozen in time. Note the arms of the king on the wooden screen.*

THE WALK

CHURCHTOWN – PARRACOMBE

The walk starts by St Petrock's Church Ⓐ, in Churchtown, on a hill above the village of Parracombe.

▶ **1** Take the path downhill, passing a house called 'Fairview' with a miniature railway in its garden.

▶ **2** When you meet a road, turn right.

▶ **3** After 200 yards (180m), turn left to cross a stile by a wooden farm gate. Go half right, heading for a path by some trees that leads you to a stile in the corner of a field. Continue along the low embankment of the dismantled railway.

▶ **4** At the lane turn right, then immediately left at the T-junction. Follow the road through the hamlet of Killington and continue until you come to the foot of a hill, where a stream runs through some meadows on the right.

▶ **5** Turn left onto a rough-surfaced track signposted 'Heddon Valley Mill'.

▶ **6** Where the path divides, just before the mill cottages, turn left onto the footpath climbing the flank of the hill.

▶ **7** At the top of the hill, go through a gate and carry on across a field, keeping to the wall on your right.

▶ **8** At the junction with an old green way Ⓑ, go straight on, following the path as it swings downhill then off to the left.

▶ **9** Turn right along the road through Bodley.

▶ **10** By a 'No Cycling' sign, turn right onto the footpath signposted to 'Tarr Path' and continue along it until you come to Parracombe.

▶ **11** At a road junction, turn left, then immediately right by a telephone box, following a 'Village Hall and

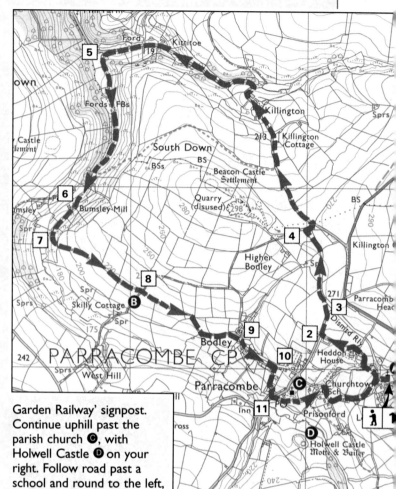

Garden Railway' signpost. Continue uphill past the parish church Ⓒ, with Holwell Castle Ⓓ on your right. Follow road past a school and round to the left, back to start of walk.

views out over the rough moorland, but as the road goes downhill it is increasingly closed in by banks and hedges. It enters a wood and is joined by a little stream alongside it.

HEDDON VALLEY

Near the foot of the hill is a ford and a footbridge, and the valley begins to open out as the stream runs through meadows bordered by reeds and brightened by marsh ragwort. Beyond it, an oak woodland rises up on the west flank of the Heddon Valley.

You turn south up this valley, along a broad track that ends at an old mill and mill cottages, now converted into holiday homes. The walk continues along a footpath that passes above the houses; beneath you, the remains of the old mill

◀ *This lovingly recreated miniature of the old Lynton and Barnstaple Railway can be seen near the start of the walk.*

pond are still visible.

This track, climbing steeply up the hill, was once the main route between the mill and Parracombe. There are faint traces of a cobbled surface and it is bordered by a stone wall, topped by mature trees. It emerges on a grassy hill with fine views, and is crossed by an old green way Ⓑ, a splendid example of roads before the invention of tarmac. The path ends at the attractive hamlet of Bodley. At the end of a short footpath, you come down to Parracombe, whose main street winds up through a narrow valley.

FROM NEW TO OLD

The final section climbs back up to Churchtown, passing a Victorian church Ⓒ, which was built in 1870 to replace — and incidentally preserve — St Petrock's. From the 'new' church there is a fine view south towards the Norman motte and bailey of Holwell Castle Ⓓ.

RAY GRANGER. INSET: PAUL STERRY/NATURE PHOTOGRAPHERS

Explore the hills and coastline of a popular holiday resort

▲ *The railway hugs the coast, running between red sandstone cliffs and the sea on its way south to Dawlish. The scaup (inset) is a marine duck that may be seen on the sea during the winter.*

Dawlish has attracted holiday-makers since the end of the 18th century. It has always had a rather genteel air, and is now a popular retirement town, though it is lively enough near the front, where the walk begins.

The town's main feature is The Lawn Ⓐ, created when sprawling Dawlish Water was straightened around 1803. The brook now flows through gardens and open spaces, and is home to ducks and black swans, introduced from Australia in 1906. Today's birds are descendants of a pair brought here in the 1940s.

The streets on either side, The Strand and Brunswick Place, were laid out at the same time as The Lawn, and soon filled with villas and boarding houses. The resort's popularity grew when the South Devon Railway came in 1846, taking a route along the Exe Estuary and the River Teign to Newton Abbot.

DECORATIVE IRONWORK

The railway Ⓑ is carried on a limestone and granite embankment above the beach, reached by a low arch by the station. Rebuilt in 1873, the station is a splendid period piece, and its excellent decorative ironwork has recently been restored.

The route follows the railway and the sea-wall towards Coryton's

FACT FILE

⚹ Dawlish, 4½ miles (7.2km) south of Exeter, on the A379

▭ Pathfinder 1342 (SX 87/97), grid reference SX 963766

miles 0 1 2 3 4 5 6 7 8 9 10 miles
kms 0 1 2 3 4 5 6 7 8 9 10 11 12 13 14 15 kms

◔ Allow 3 hours

▬ Surfaced paths, lanes and promenades and good field paths. Two fairly steep climbs on Lea Mount and Empson's Hill. Care needed on sections of sea-wall in bad weather or at high tides

Ⓟ Pay and display car parks at the west end of The Lawn

Ⓣ BR Intercity from Paddington to Plymouth and Cornwall; local train services from Newton Abbot and Exeter

🍺🍴 Many pubs, cafés and restaurants in Dawlish; seasonal snack bar at Langstone Rock

[WC] Barton Hill, at the west end of The Lawn, and by Big Red Rock

Ⓘ The Tourist Information Centre on The Lawn has details of tide times, Tel. (01626) 863589

Cove, then begins a winding climb up the sandstone cliffs. The cliffs, banded by layers of breccia, a type of compounded gravel, have been shaped and smoothed by the wind. At the top is Lea Mount Ⓒ, a small park with splendid views north over the town and, from under a lone Scots pine, south along the coast towards Thatcher Rock off Torbay.

Barton Lane, an old footpath, which now runs between high garden walls, leads to the churchyard Ⓓ nearly 1 mile (1.6km) inland. This is the heart of the old village, which supported itself through pilchard fishing, basket-making, salt production, and a little smuggling.

The church was largely rebuilt in the 19th century; only the red sandstone tower remains of the medieval building. Beyond the lychgate is the New Hay, a glebe field where bare-knuckle fights were staged. Alongside the field is a leat that once served the town's mill.

SEA VIEWS

A fairly strenuous climb to the top of Empson's Hill Ⓔ is rewarded by views south over Dawlish to the sea, and north over farmland to the Exe. Inland, wooded hills rise gently towards the tors of Dartmoor.

The route follows a footpath and a residential street back to the seafront. A short walk along the sea-wall (closed at high tide) leads to a clifftop section of the South West Coast Path. Beside the track, seabirds sail by at eye level and there are glimpses ahead of the Exe

THE WALK

DAWLISH – DAWLISH WARREN

The walk begins at the seaward end of The Lawn Ⓐ, beside the railway bridge.

1 ► Cross the road and go under the bridge. Turn immediately right up a ramp and along the sea-wall by the railway Ⓑ. Just before the wall ends at Coryton's Cove, turn sharp right up some steps and along a steep, paved path. At the fork, go up the steps to the left. Continue uphill to a crossing path.

2 ► Turn left to the viewpoint at Lea Mount Ⓒ. Retrace your steps, with the railing to your right. Do not turn right, downhill; go straight ahead to a road. Turn right, then left down Barton Lane, an alley opening to the right of Westcliff Road. Follow this for just over ½ mile (800m) to its end. Turn right, then right again at a T-junction. After about 20 yards (18m), take the signposted footpath to your left through a kissing-gate into the churchyard Ⓓ. Go ahead to the left of the tower, through the lychgate, then immediately left. Continue ahead over a brook to a road.

3 ► Turn right and go over the bridge. Take the third of three right turns in quick succession, and begin to climb. Near the top, a road marked 'Private Road — The Humpty' turns off right. About 40 yards (36m) further up, go right on a gravel path, then ahead over a stile and along the field edge. Go through a gate, turn left for 30 yards (27m), then right over a step stile. Follow the hedge to your right to a stile by the fir trees at the top of Empson's Hill Ⓔ. Continue ahead, with the hedge on your left, over a stile and down along an enclosed footpath.

4 ► At the road, turn left, then right down Wallace Avenue. Continue downhill to a T-junction with the main road. Cross and go through a gap in the wall. Bear left, downhill. Go over the footbridge and left along the sea-wall to the next footbridge over the railway line. (Note: the wall between the bridges is impassable at high tide; check the tide times before starting, or continue along the main road and rejoin the route near the start of stage 5.)

5 ► Cross the bridge. Bear left past some wooden benches, then turn sharp right between a wire fence on your right and a wall on your left. Follow this path up to and along the clifftop, then down through trees, past a hotel, and into the trees again. A car park opens on your right. Turn right through the gate at the far end and over a railway footbridge ahead.

6 ► Turn right. Follow the line past Langstone Rock Ⓕ on your left. Either follow the sea-wall or go down the steps and walk along the beach back to the start.

and of the red cliffs on the far shore.

The path leads down to the outskirts of Dawlish Warren, a modern resort of chalets, camps and caravans for boisterous family holidays. Beyond the shops and sideshows, protected by large breakwaters, is the Warren itself, a sand spit stretching more than 1 mile (1.6km) across the mouth of the Exe. Its further reaches are wild and lonely, with a 55-acre (22-hectare) wildlife reserve. Over 180 species of bird can be seen here in a year, and there are more than 450 flowering plants.

The best views of the Warren are from the footbridge taking the route back to the shore, or from Langstone Rock Ⓕ, an outlying headland separated from the main cliffs by a sweeping curve of the railway. It is worth scrambling to the top for the sake of the vantage point, used in the past by customs men seeking out smugglers and wreckers.

From here, you can return either along the sea-wall or on the beach, where, at low tide, the flat, red sand and gravel make easy walking all the way back to the start.

RAY GRANGER

► *The winding footpath up to Lea Mount provides good views of the sandstone cliffs and stacks.*

THE CAMEL TRAIL

JONATHAN PLANT. INSET: C. A. HILL/NATURE PHOTOGRAPHERS

Along the route of the old Bodmin and Wadebridge Railway

The hamlet of Helland is little more than a scatter of houses dominated by the granite tower of the parish church. The church seems surprisingly large for such a small place, but it serves a wide community of farms and other hamlets.

From Helland there is a view across to the wooded hills on the opposite side of the Camel Valley. The grey patches among the greenery are tongues of spoil from old quarry workings. The single track road down the hill towards Hellandbridge is typically Cornish with very high banks on either side. The road sinks ever deeper as it goes downhill until the stony banks themselves reach well above head height and are then topped by stunted trees and hedgerows.

Hellandbridge, at the bottom of the hill, is an attractive group of

FACT FILE

☀ Helland, 2½ miles (4 km) north of Bodmin

🄾🅂 Pathfinder 1338 (SX 07/17), grid reference SX 075710

miles 0 1 2 3 4 5 6 7 8 9 10 miles
kms 0 1 2 3 4 5 6 7 8 9 10 11 12 13 14 15 kms

◔ Allow 2 hrs

▬ Mostly easy walking with one moderately steep hill. The Camel Trail is also very popular with cyclists

🅿 In side road by Helland church

🍺 Pub at Blisland

🍴 Cafés, pubs and toilets in Bodmin

stone cottages. Although the walk now turns onto the disused railway, it is worth walking on a short distance to see the attractive medieval stone bridge across the River Camel **Ⓐ**. The narrow roadway has passing places created above the massive

▲ *The Camel Trail follows the path of the first Cornish passenger steam railway, opened in 1834. The nocturnal tawny owl (inset) swoops silently on small mammals, its main prey.*

supporting piers of the old bridge.

The Camel Trail **Ⓑ** itself is based on the track bed of the old Bodmin and Wadebridge Railway. Designed by a Cornishman, Henry Taylor, this was the first railway built in Cornwall for the use of steam locomotives, though it was not joined to the rest of the network until 1886.

RIVER VIEW

The trail is named after the River Camel whose valley the old railway line used to follow. It has much the same character as a country lane, with banks and hedgerows on either side. Shortly after joining the walk, look out for one of the old railway distance stones to the right of the path. After leaving the shallow cutting, the path enters woodland and the river, which up to now has only been heard gurgling behind the

THE WALK

HELLAND AND THE RIVER CAMEL

The walk starts by Helland church.

▶**1** At the T-junction, with the church behind you, turn left and take the road downhill for about ¾ mile (1.2 km).

▶**2** At the foot of the hill continue on the road as it bends round to the right towards the River Camel Ⓐ.

▶**3** At the railway crossing, turn right onto the Camel Trail Ⓑ.

▶**4** By the signpost to Poley's Bridge, cross the stile by the car park and take the road up through the woods.

▶**5** About 200 yards (180 metres) before the top of the hill you will see the driveway to

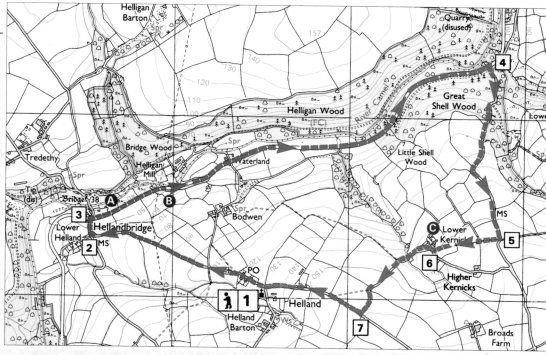

Coldrenick on your left, marked by stone gateposts. Opposite this is a very high stone stile signed 'public footpath'. Go over the stile and through the field, with the hedge on your left, to a farm track. Go left, then immediately right

and continue in the same direction with the hedge on your right. Make for the gate to the right of the farmhouse across the field to your left. If the stile is overgrown and impassable, continue to the top of the hill and turn right, as signposted,

to Helland.

▶**6** At the roadway, turn right. Pass through Lower Kernick Ⓒ, following the road as it bears to the left.

▶**7** At the T-junction turn right and return to Helland.

BOTH PHOTOS JONATHAN PLANT

trees, comes into view. The track itself runs on a little ledge cut into the rock of the hillside and is overhung by trees. The old railway was built more or less straight, but the river bends and twists, sometimes running alongside the trail then swinging away again.

By the traditional stone farmhouse 'Waterland', there are wider views across the valley to the steep, heavily-wooded slopes on the opposite bank. On the near side of the river, green fields run down to the

◀*Note the massive supporting pillars of this medieval stone bridge, which spans the River Camel.*

track. Shrubs and trees line the route; elder, beech, birch and dog rose are well established and blackberries grow in profusion. A thin line of oak woodland straddles a small stream, which meets the line just before the path itself enters Shell Wood — an area of mixed pine and broad-leaved woodland. Here the path passes through an avenue of oak while the river rushes through a series of small falls. Look out for the pathside benches which are made out of old railway sleepers.

GLORIOUS BANKS

After leaving the Camel Trail, the walk joins the lane that climbs uphill through the wood, between high banks. These are seen at their best in spring and early summer

▶*Part of the walk leads through the verdant Camel Valley, which includes Shell Wood.*

when they are a mass of flowers.

Across the fields is Lower Kernick Ⓒ, where the farm is built in the typical style of the area, with slate-hung walls. From here, there are particularly good views back across the Camel Valley.

A waterfall and hill-top views on the flanks of Snowdon

The village of Llanberis, at the foot of Snowdon, teems with walkers ready to tackle the paths that climb towards the 3,560-foot (1,085-m) peak of the mountain. This walk is less ambitious: its goal is a hill fort just 1,076 feet (328m) above sea level, a total ascent of 728 feet (222m). There is still much inspiring scenery, though, as you pass a fine waterfall and look back down the rocky slopes to the lakes below.

MOUNTAIN RAILWAY

The walk begins at the terminus of the Snowdon Mountain Railway **A**. Completed in 1896, this is the only rack railway in Britain. The track, which you follow in the initial stages of the walk, has a narrow gauge of 2 feet 7½ inches (80cm).

The line goes all the way to the summit, but you part company with it soon after the Ceunant Mawr waterfall **B**. Llyn Padarn (Llyn is Welsh for lake) occupies the bottom

▲*In fine weather, this hill walk is an exhilarating one, enlivened by lovely views. From damp hollows you may put up a snipe (inset), which will fly swiftly away in a zigzag line.*

FACT FILE

- ☀ Llanberis, 6 miles (9.6km) from Caernarfon

- 🗺 Outdoor Leisure Map 17, grid reference SH 582597

  miles 0 1 2 3 4 5 6 7 8 9 10 miles
  kms 0 1 2 3 4 5 6 7 8 9 10 11 12 13 14 15 kms

- ◕ Allow 2 hours

- ⬛ Steady ascents and descents on good paths and tracks

- **P** Car parks signposted in Llanberis

- **T** Buses from Llandudno (seasonal), Bangor (weekdays) and Caernarfon (Mon-Sat). Snowdonia Mountain Railway terminus (summer)

- 🍴 Pubs and cafés in Llanberis

- **I** Tourist information (summer) in Llanberis, Tel. (01286) 713177

of a valley that was hollowed out and deepened by a glacier in the last Ice Age. The mountain streams that now run into it cascade down the steep sides from hanging valleys.

The falls of Ceunant Mawr are created by the little Afon Arddu. There are actually two separate falls; the first is a 40-foot (12-m) plunge into a pool, and the second an 80-foot (24-m) oblique, angled slide down a rock face.

You continue the steady climb a little further, then follow roads and tracks across the slopes towards the

▼*Leaving Llanberis terminus, the attractive rolling stock of the Snowdon Mountain Railway crosses a viaduct.*

THE WALK

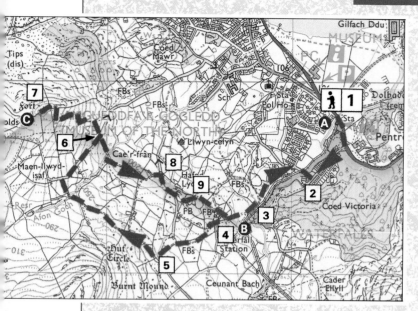

LLANBERIS – DINAS TY-DU

The walk begins at the lower terminus of the Snowdon Mountain Railway Ⓐ, *on the A4086 just to the south of Llanberis.*

▶ With your back to the station, turn right along the road. Opposite the Royal Victoria Hotel, turn right up Victoria Terrace.

▶ Turn right up a road signposted to the waterfalls. Go under the railway viaduct and first left up a lane.

▶ Go past some cottages on your right, then through a small gate in the wall on your left. Cross the railway with care to enjoy a view of Ceunant Mawr waterfall Ⓑ. Return to the lane and continue to climb. After nearly 50 yards (45m), fork right. After 100 yards (90m), bear left through a kissing-gate.

▶ Follow a grassy path through a gap in the wall ahead. Bear right, keeping the wall to your right. Cross a stream in the corner of the field. Turn right through a small metal gate, and follow the stream across a field. Go ahead through another gate and walk with the wall on your left to a road.

▶ Turn left, then go right along a track to a T-junction with another road. Turn right.

▶ After ¾ mile (1.2km), when a track appears on your right, turn left through a gate. Follow the zigzag path up to the hill fort Ⓒ at the summit.

▶ Retrace your steps to the road, and then follow the track opposite to another road.

▶ Turn right. When the road bends to the right, continue ahead through a kissing-gate. Go through a gate in the wall opposite, and follow the wall on your left to a ruin in the trees. Turn left towards the lake, and continue until you reach a small metal gate in the lower wall.

▶ Go through the gate and turn right. Bear right around the back of Crochendy Pottery and through a kissing-gate. Turn left to retrace your steps to the start.

▲ *The Afon Arddu, reinforced by the waters of Afon Hwch, tumbles some 120 feet (36m) at Ceunant Mawr. Beyond this you encounter views of a rugged, farmed landscape (right).*

Iron Age hill fort of Dinas Ty-du (Black House City) Ⓒ, reached by a winding, sometimes rough path. There is very little here to remind you of the past, just a few scattered stones; the point of the visit, though, is the view from the site.

Llanberis is set out below you, with Llyn Padarn to its left and Llyn Peris to its right. On the slopes to the north there are the grey scars of the old slate quarries, some of which have now found use as reservoirs, while the mountains fill the horizons in all directions save the west, where you can see across to Anglesey and the Irish Sea.

WALLED FIELDS

The descent tracks across the slopes lower down, heading through a network of small, walled fields, before rejoining the outward route just above the waterfall.

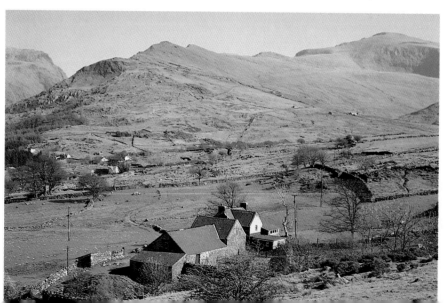

WELSHPOOL

24

WALES

Through the wildlife corridor of a canal and castle parkland

Welshpool is an ancient town that now forms the gateway to Wales for visitors from the English Midlands. It must give an attractive first impression, with its half-timbered buildings and places to visit. Time will be at a premium, with the canal, the castle and the light railway all vying for your attention. This fairly gentle walk takes you to all three and brings some relaxing views over the rolling

FACT FILE

- ✱ Welshpool, Powys, at the junction of the A458 and A483

- os Pathfinder 888 (SJ 20/30), grid reference SJ 225075

- miles 0 1 2 3 4 5 6 7 8 9 10 miles
  kms 0 1 2 3 4 5 6 7 8 9 10 11 12 13 14 15 kms

- ◐ Allow 3 hours, plus plenty of time for visits

- ▬ Fairly gentle. Mostly towpath, quiet lanes, woodland paths and parkland drive

- P A car park is near the start

- WC Behind the Tourist Information Centre

- 🍴 Pubs, cafés, restaurants and shops in Welshpool

- I Powysland Museum: Monday, Tuesday, Thursday, Friday, 11am-1pm, 2-5pm, and in summer (Whitsun-September) Saturday & Sunday 10am-1pm, 2-5pm, winter Saturday 2-5pm. Montgomery Canal Centre boat trips: Tel. (01938) 553271

- ⌂ Powis Castle and Museum: April-June and September-October, daily except Monday and Tuesday; July-August, daily except Monday, 12-5pm (garden 11am-6pm)

ALL PHOTOS JEREMY MOORE

▶ *The Montgomeryshire Canal was once a thriving industrial waterway, carrying limestone and coal to make fertilizer. The barges (right) moored outside the Canal Centre are now used for pleasure.*

countryside of the former county of Montgomeryshire.

The Tourist Information Centre at the start of the walk is built on the site of the old track of the Welshpool and Llanfair Light Railway when it used to clank through the town, crossing Church Street **Ⓐ**. From 1903 to 1956, the fireman would get down from his engine to stop the traffic in Church Street with a red flag before the train went across. More dramatic, on 14th June 1886, was the murder of William Mabbot at No 6 Church Street. Strychnine poisoning, it was reported, brought about a quick death and William Samuels was soon swinging at the end of a rope on 26th July 1886 in Shrewsbury jail.

The Powysland Museum and Montgomeryshire Canal Centre **Ⓑ** is housed in a converted canal-side warehouse. The history of the area, from prehistoric days up until the 20th century, is expertly portrayed here. The Montgomeryshire Canal

THE WALK

WELSHPOOL

The walk begins at the Tourist Information Centre just off Church Street in Welshpool. A car park is nearby.

▶**1** Go right to Church Street **A** and turn left down it, passing the Spar shop on your left. Reach The Cross and turn left along Severn Street. Come to a bridge over a canal. Visit the Powysland Museum and Montgomeryshire Canal Centre **B** on your right, then cross the bridge.

▶**2** Turn left to walk along the towpath beside the canal on your left. Pass under an old railway girder bridge **C**, then continue under a new bridge.

▶**3** Go ahead across a road at Gallowstree Bank **D**. Resume walking along the towpath beside the canal on your left. Pass under one bridge, then reach a second bridge.

▶**4** Go up the steps on your right before this bridge and turn left across it. Notice Buttington Wharf **E** on your right. Go straight ahead along a lane, bearing right at a fork.

▶**5** Turn left at a crossroads. Pass Caethro **F** on your left and go left when the road forks to go towards Coed-y-wlad **G**. Pass Sheridan Grange and a drive on your left. Follow the road to a T-junction.

▶**6** Take the road on your left for about 60 yards (54 metres), then turn right over a wood bar stile to enter the corner of a field. Go ahead with a hedge on your right.

▶**7** Cross a stile beside a gate and turn left. Walk with a fence on your left and a stream in a dingle on your right. Go over a stile to follow the path down through Bron-y-Buckley Wood **H**. At the far end of this wood, follow the path that bears left beside a hedge on your right.

▶**8** Emerge on an estate road and go left along it for 20 yards (18 metres). Turn right at a mini-roundabout to descend and cross a lower road. Continue in this direction to reach the High Street. If you wish to divert to the Welshpool and Llanfair Light Railway **J**, go right to its terminus at Raven Square. Going left along the High Street, pass Park Lane House **K** on your right and turn right up Park Street. Go through the gate to Powis Castle **L**.

▶**9** Retrace your steps to the High Street, noticing Christ Church **M** on your left. Turn right, pass the Town Hall **N** on the left, then turn left up Hall Street. Go right to reach St Mary's church and see Grace Evans' Cottage just after it. Go right to return to the start.

connected the industrial potential of Newtown with the Llangollen Canal at Frankton Junction. In 1821, upon completion, it was about 35 miles (56 km) long. The advent of the railways led to its decline and the canal was officially abandoned in 1944. The threat of its loss under a proposed by-pass reminded the locals of their neglected asset and this section of the canal was restored in 1969. The girder bridge **C** used to carry the Welshpool and Llanfair Light Railway to its terminus beside the main line station.

GALLOWS

The canal is piped under the A483 at Gallowstree Bank **D**. This name refers to the fact that Welshpool's gallows once stood here. Reeds make the canal an attractive haven for wildlife and waterfowl today.

Buttington Wharf **E** was a major centre for the lime-burning industry, which was the mainstay of the Montgomeryshire Canal. Limestone was brought from quarries above

▶ *This old stone bridge spans the waters of the Montgomeryshire Canal between Gallowstree Bank and Buttington Wharf.*

which means 'trees in the wild'. Bron-y-Buckley Wood **H** has survived above a dingle famous for its fossils. The trees are mostly beech.

Enjoy a ride on the Welshpool and Llanfair Light Railway **J** from Raven Square to Llanfair Caereinion, 9 miles (14.4km) to the west. Steam-hauled trains run regularly from Easter to the end of September (Tel. [01938] 810441 for full details). Two steam engines have survived since the opening of this line in 1903 (it closed temporarily between 1956 and 1963) and others have been brought to join them on the 2 ft 6 in guage track.

Welshpool's High Street is full of interesting old buildings. One of these, No 31, houses the office of the Campaign for the Protection of Rural Wales (Cymru Wledig). Across the street is a 16th-century, timber-framed structure, No 11; and

Llanymynech and coal came from Ruabhon. Unloaded by hand at the wharf, it was tipped into the tops of the three limekilns to be carried to local farms by horse and cart. In 1830, when the acid upland soils were first brought into cultivation, 2,000 tons of lime were burnt here.

Caethro **F** is derived from Cae Athro, meaning 'the field of the schoolmaster'. All this land was once covered by oak trees, as indicated by the name Coed-y-wlad **G**,

◀ *The site of Christ Church was once used for less sacred activities — an old market and a fairground. Grace Evans' Cottage (below) was her reward for her role in a daring jailbreak.*

Nos 9 and 10 were already standing when the building was recorded as the town house of Kynaston the Wild during the reign of Henry VIII (1509-47). Another old house is The Butter (No 8). It was formerly the Cross Keys Inn and stage coaches used to run from here. Park Lane House **K** is at No 7 and is a listed building of the Regency style.

If you have ever been to the Robber's Grave in the churchyard at

Montgomery note that the magistrate who committed the innocent man to the gallows lived here. It is now an art gallery.

FORTRESS FORTUNES

The highlight of this walk is Powis Castle **L**, so divert along the drive to see this fortress-turned-mansion. In 1274, Gwynedd's Llewelyn the Last razed the fortress of Gruffudd the son of Gwenwynwyn, Prince of Powys, to the ground. Eventually, in 1286, Owain, the son of Gruffudd, acknowledged the English conquest of Wales by renouncing the title of Prince of Powys and paying homage to Edward I as Baron de la Pole. The new surname was derived from the name of the town, Poole. Because of the existence of a Poole in Dorset, the town soon became known as Welshpool. The newly created baron was also responsible for the building of the then new Powis Castle.

Christ Church **M** was built in the 19th century on the site of the old market and fairground. The Town Hall **N** was completed in 1804 and enlarged in 1873. It has avoided the fate of its predecessors whose floors would regularly give way during trials. Six spectators were trampled to death when this happened to the old Hall during the Court of Great Session in 1758.

Grace Evans' Cottage, passed near the end of the walk, was given to Grace, a lady-in-waiting of Lady Nithsdale, when she returned to Welshpool from France in 1735. The cottage was Grace's reward for the part she played in helping to secure the escape of Lord Nithsdale from the Tower of London in 1716, just two days before the date fixed for his execution on 24th February. The Jacobite Lord Nithsdale escaped, dressed as a woman, in the company of his wife, who was one of the daughters of the Marquis of Powis.

▶ *The rolling countryside seen on this walk is typical of much of this part of Montgomeryshire.*

Powis Castle

What began as a fortress was turned into a sumptuous mansion by later residents. Sir Edward Herbert, second son of the first Earl of Pembroke, acquired the property in 1587. His wife was a Roman Catholic and the family supported the Stuarts. They celebrated the restoration of Charles II with the installation of a magnificent State Bedroom and the

The beautiful red sandstone of this sumptuous fortress-turned-mansion glows warmly in the evening sun, as it has done for 700 years.

Wales is famous for its castles, most of which were built by the invading Edward I to contain the Welsh. These are found mostly in Gwynedd, encircling Snowdonia, at places like Conwy, Harlech and Caernarfon. The people of Powys had no mountain fortress to retreat to and were only the width of Offa's Dyke from the English. The princes of Powys were, therefore, more pragmatic than the independent-minded rulers of Gwynedd. Instead of resisting the English, they absorbed them and any conflict was more likely between the ruling houses of Gwynedd and Powys.

construction of the spectacular, terraced gardens, begun in the late 16th century and completed in the next century by Capability Brown. Some of the terraces are 200 yards (182 metres) long and drop down in four stages to a lawn. There are also many fine examples of statues and topiary. The gardens contain a huge variety of trees and shrubs, including a Douglas fir, which at 181 feet (55 metres) is thought to be the tallest tree in Britain. In 1784 Lady Henrietta Herbert married Edward Clive, the eldest son of Clive of India. The Clive fortune paid for repairs to the castle and improvements to the garden and park. Its striking interior features are the panelled Elizabethan Long Gallery, the Blue Drawing Room, the State Bedroom, the Grand Staircase, the Dining Room and the Oak Drawing Room. The fine collection of old master pictures, Indian curiosities and French and English furniture is another result of this marriage. The Herberts, who had been created Earls of Powis in 1748, bequeathed this fine red sandstone castle to the National Trust in 1952.

The magnificent Grand Staircase, with its cleverly deceptive trompe l'oeil decoration, is one of the many jewels of Powis Castle.

CWM RHEIDOL

falls and the beautiful wooded dingles... you must be a very unpoetical person indeed'. But it was to be another 40 years before mass tourism really came to this area with the construction of a railway. The local lead mines welcomed a line down to the port,

◄*Afon Mynach tumbles some 300 feet (90 metres) over a spectacular series of waterfalls. Toy kites are named after the red kite (below) because of the bird's hovering and gliding habit.*

HELLIO & VAN INGEN/NHPA

JANET & COLIN BORD/WALES SCENE

A walk through oak-clad slopes and over prehistoric moorland

Of all the vales in Wales, the Vale of Rheidol is arguably the most attractive. Its chief asset is its steep slopes clad in native sessile oaks. The view through these trees makes a ride on the steam train from Aberystwyth a memorable experience. Countless visitors have come to the Vale of Rheidol to marvel at the dramatic falls below Devil's Bridge, as did Wordsworth in 1824. He was astounded that: 'such a force of waters issue from a British source'. The falls are the meeting place of the Rheidol and Mynach and are best seen from below. Here is spectacular scenery,

wildlife in abundance, enigmatic remains from prehistory and a famous legend.

The walk begins on Devil's Bridge **Ⓐ**. This is a place to provide for generously, both in time and money. A visit to its nature trail could extend this walk by well over an hour, while the turnstiles for both this and the Devil's Punchbowl will make demands on your purse.

THE AGE OF THE TRAIN

Strangely, one of the place's most famous visitors, George Borrow (the author of *Wild Wales*, 1862), seemed more interested in the band of young robbers, known as the Plant de Bat, who used to live in a cave here rather than in the story of the bridge itself. However, he wrote that 'if pleasant recollections do not haunt you through life of the noble

FACT FILE

- ☀ Devil's Bridge, Dyfed, 12 miles (19.2 km) east of Aberystwyth, on the A4120

- 🗺 Pathfinder 947 (SN 67/77), grid reference SN 741770

  miles 0 1 2 3 4 5 6 7 8 9 10 miles
  kms 0 1 2 3 4 5 6 7 8 9 10 11 12 13 14 15 kms

- 🕐 Allow 4½ hours

- ▬ Moderately strenuous, along steep valley paths and over high moorland

- P A car park is signposted up the road between the Devil's Bridge and the Hafod Arms

- T Steam-hauled trains operate on the Vale of Rheidol Railway from Aberystwyth during the season, Tel. (01970) 625819. Buses 538 and 596 depart from Aberystwyth

- 🍴 In Devil's Bridge, either at the Hafod Arms or at the railway
- WC station

THE WALK

DEVIL'S BRIDGE – PARSON'S BRIDGE

The walk begins from the famous Devil's Bridge Ⓐ, near which is a car park.

1 Take the road into the village, passing the Hafod Arms on your left and the upper terminus of the Vale of Rheidol Railway Ⓑ on your right. Pass 'Fronhaul', the last bungalow in the village, on your right.

2 Turn right through a gate and go ahead to the top of the Rheidol Gorge. Bear left, ignoring a fork down to a gate on your right. Continue ahead through trees and eventually descend to a small gate in a corner near the railway. Continue through another gate to turn right across the track carefully. Enter the National Nature Reserve Ⓒ and go left to emerge over a stile back to the railway. Do not cross, but turn right to walk with care beside the track until you reach the stump of an old stile just before conifer trees on your right.

3 Turn right down steps and through the conifers. Bear left when you reach a lower track. Continue across open hillside, overlooking the old Cwm Rheidol mine workings Ⓓ on your right. Go through a gate to bear right down to the river.

4 Cross the footbridge, go left for about 20 yards (18 metres) and take the uphill path signposted on your right. Continue upwards across two tracks, as waymarked. Climbing to the next waymarked path, turn right to ascend with it.

5 Pass a ruin and turn left immediately to climb above it and go right as waymarked. Gradually ascend through the oak trees to a higher waymarked path and go right. Continue above conifers on your right and fork left, as waymarked. Reach a waymark post above the trees, go ahead to a second post and bear left as marked. Cross a stile and walk beside a fence, then a wall, on your right. Go ahead over stiles to a lane.

6 Go right, ignoring the lane to Ystumtuen youth hostel on your right, and pass a second lane on your right. Just before a bungalow on your left, take a gate on your right. Bear left to cross a stile and climb past the shafts of an old mine Ⓔ. Pass a reservoir on your left and go ahead over stiles and down to a waymark post. Divert to the Temple Cairn Stone Circle Ⓕ on your left.

7 Return to the waymark post and go downhill over two stiles, to cross the river by Parson's Bridge Ⓖ. Zigzag uphill to the top of the valley and follow the path to the church of St John Ⓗ at Ysbyty Cynfyn.

8 Go right along the verge of the road for 1 mile (1.6 km). Pass a farm on your left, followed by a lay-by on your left, then bear left through a gate and follow power lines up a field. Cross a stile, veer left to a gate. Go through the gate and then turn right. Follow a track through two gates and veer left to cross a stile in the upper fence at a corner.

9 Veer right to cross a broken stile into woodland and turn right. Bear left at a track and keep beside the fence on your right. Cross a stile beside a gate, go ahead to a footbridge at the site of Bodcoll Woollen Mill Ⓙ and cross it to bear right to a road.

10 Cross the road to take the gate opposite. Bear right along a track, taking a gate ahead to pass trees on your right, then turn sharply right along the base of the trees. Pass a sheep market on your right and cross a stile to take its access track to the road. The railway station is facing you, while the Devil's Bridge and its car park, where you started from, are on your right.

◄*Steam train enthusiasts should park in Aberystwyth and take the Vale of Rheidol Railway. Sessile oaks (right) are abundant in Coed Rheidol, the National Nature Reserve.*

but when work started on laying the 1 foot 11½-inch (60-cm) gauge track in 1901, it was with the transport of tourists from Aberystwyth in mind. The 12 miles (19.2 km) of line had an average gradient of 1:48.

The Vale of Rheidol Railway Ⓑ

opened for goods traffic in August, 1902, with the first passenger trains running that Christmas. The lead mines were virtually dead by 1914 and the last freight train ran in 1926. Tourist traffic was encouraged by the provision of a charabanc to carry passengers from the Devil's Bridge terminus right up Plynlimon. When the Great Western Railway acquired the line in 1922, they invested in two new engines, *Owain Glyndwr* and *Llewelyn*. These still pull the trains, along with the rebuilt original company's *Prince of Wales*. The *Lein Bach* was sold by British Rail to the Brecon Mountain Railway in 1989.

The National Nature Reserve Ⓒ is

DEREK FORSS

CELTIC PICTURE AGENCY

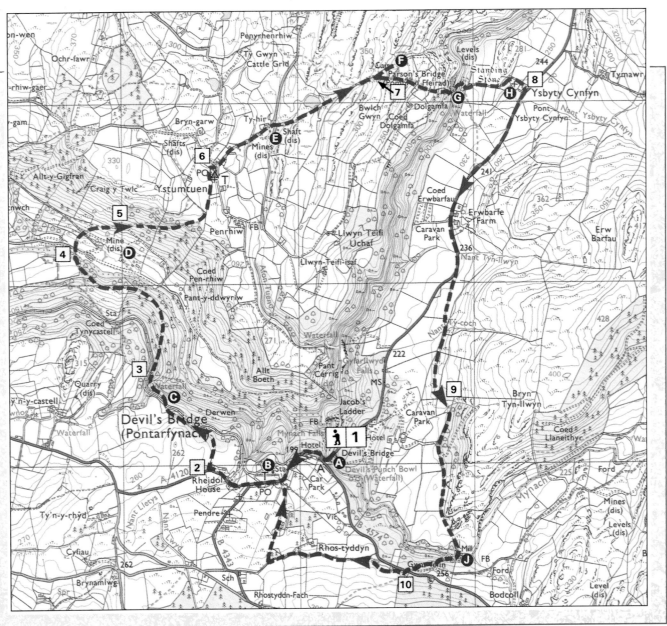

formed mainly of sessile or Durmast oaks. Sessile, meaning stalkless, refers to the fact that the acorns sit tightly on the twigs without stalks. These trees covered most of the Welsh hills below 2,000 feet (609 metres). Very few Welsh valleys have retained their trees, however, because of farming but the sides of this gorge have defied the plough and the encroachment of sheep.

MINES AND MEGALITHS

The Cwm Rheidol lead mine **D** was connected to the railway by an aerial ropeway. More lead mines **E** are passed at Ystumtuen. Active from the 17th century to about 1900, the lead mines were served by the reservoir passed on this walk.

Ancient man valued these uplands too. The Temple Cairn Circle **F** may not be in the same league as Stonehenge or Avebury,

▶ *The minerals in the lead deposits, which made this area a profitable mining centre, colour the water bright orange.*

but it is significant. Its dimensions confirm the use of Professor Thom's megalithic yard. This circle was built using one quarter of such a measurement as the basic unit. The perimeter is 16 megalithic yards, while the short axis is 4¾ megalithic yards. The foci of the ellipse are 2¾ megalithic yards apart, while the long axis is exactly twice this. Curiously, the Nine Stones at Winterbourne Abbas in Dorset form a ring exactly twice this size, with a similar grading in height of the individual stones.

Parson's Bridge **G** refers to the place where the local parson had to cross the deep-cutting River Rheidol between Ystumtuen and Ysbyty Cynfyn. It used to be a swaying

Margaret, Elizabeth, Catherine and Isaac, died within six days of their birth to Margaret Hughes on 17th February 1856. Typhoid was rampant and their elder brother, Hugh, joined them on 1st March 1856, followed by their father, Isaac Hughes (aged 32) on 6th March and his daughter Hannah (aged 3) on 10th March. Only the mother survived.

Although there is not much to see now, Bodcoll Woollen Mill **J** was active in the 18th and 19th centuries. It was fed by water taken upstream of the nearby miniature gorge.

◀*The Temple Cairn Circle confirms prehistoric man's use of very precise measurements, according to modern calculations, in his building projects.*

plank that hung from the sides of the gorge by chains until the present bridge was built in 1951.

TYPHOID TRAGEDY

The church of St John **H**, Ysbyty Cynfyn is where the first boundary hospice awaited pilgrims travelling to Strata Florida Abbey. 'Ysbyty' means hospice in Welsh. It may possibly be set within an ancient stone circle. Look too for some sad graves next to the railing around a yew tree to your left as you face the church porch. The graves include the first record of quadruplets. All four,

▼*The Ten Commandments, the Creed and the Lord's Prayer are inscribed in Welsh in Ysbyty Cynfyn church.*

A Bridge 'Built by the Devil'

The original Devil's Bridge is now beneath two later structures, but it can be seen by entering the nature trail (for which there is a charge). Dating from, perhaps, 1087, it is thrown across a chasm 118 feet (36 metres) above the River Mynach as it plunges over 300 feet (91 metres) in a series of waterfalls towards the River Rheidol. (A second bridge was built on top of it in 1708, to be followed by a third in 1901.)

In the Middle Ages only the devil was deemed capable of such a construction, although he had to be 'disguised as a monk' to fit the fact that such works were actually the labour of monks.

The legend is that an old woman called Marged lived near the ravine. One day her cow managed to cross to the other side. In despair, Marged cried she would give anything to have a bridge to fetch the cow home.

Suddenly, a figure in the habit of a Cistercian monk appeared and began to build the bridge. Telling Marged to go home until it was completed, he named his price as the soul of the first living thing to cross the bridge.

After just one hour, Marged was amazed to hear him call her to see the finished bridge. She rushed out with some bread in her hand and her dog at her heels. As she was about to cross, Marged noticed that the monk had horns and cloven hooves. He was the devil after her soul! With

quick thinking, she threw her bread across the bridge and let her dog run after it. The devil was so enraged at this trick that he immediately disappeared in a puff of smoke.

The triple spans of the bridges can be seen from the Devil's Punchbowl. The original bridge is the one at the bottom.

The view from the top of Constitution Hill is spectacular on a clear day. Sea campion (inset) is common on the cliff tops.

WALES

octagonal tower in which the admission charge brings you the services of a 14-inch (35-cm) lens system to focus detailed views on a screen in a darkened viewing gallery.

IRON AGE HILLFORT

After Penglais Woods, there is a view across Aberystwyth. From here you can also see the monument on the top of Pen Dinas, the Iron Age hillfort south of the town. This is shaped like a canon barrel and was erected in 1852 in memory of the Duke of Wellington.

The buildings of the university at the top of the hill on your left are a reminder of the 100,000 or more small donations, from coal mines and chapels, that paid for the establishment of this seat of learning. Part of it is still located in the hotel on the sea front, which was bought at a bargain price from a speculator and became the University College of Aberystwyth in 1872.

One of its most notable students was Prince Charles who came here to study Welsh in 1969 before his

A walk along the cliff tops then through woods above Aberystwyth

Choose a clear day to enjoy the views from the cliff-top path and Aberystwyth on the way back. There is a stiff climb up Constitution Hill, but you could avoid this by taking the Cliff Railway.

The view from the top extends from Strumble Head in the south to Bardsey Island, off the tip of the Lleyn Peninsula, in the north. After overlooking the valley of the River Clarach, you return through attractive oak woodland.

The Tourist Information Centre is next to the Ceredigion Museum Ⓐ, which is housed in the restored Edwardian Coliseum Theatre.

Having walked past the beach you may be tempted by the Cliff Railway Ⓑ up Constitution Hill. A small fee will save you the 400-foot (120-metre) climb if you go between 10am and 6pm from Easter to October. The longest electric cliff railway in Great Britain, it leads to the Camera Obscura Ⓒ. This is an

FACT FILE

✳ Aberystwyth, Dyfed

▭ Pathfinder 926 (SN57/58), grid reference SN 583818

miles 0 1 2 3 4 5 6 7 8 9 10 miles
kms 0 1 2 3 4 5 6 7 8 9 10 11 12 13 14 15 kms

◔ Allow 2½ hours

▭ Easy, except for the steep climb up Constitution Hill, which can be avoided by taking the Cliff Railway in season. Good walking shoes are highly recommended

Ⓟ Car park opposite the Tourist Information Centre near the sea front in the centre of the town (signposted)

Ⓣ Trains and buses to the station, from where you take Ffordd y Mor (Terrace Road) towards the sea

ᵂᶜ Toilets and refreshments in Aberystwyth and at the top of Constitution Hill (in season)

▶ *Aberystwyth's electric cliff railway is the longest in the country and saves the steep climb up Constitution Hill.*

CELTIC PICTURE LIBRARY. INSET: MARTIN KING/SWIFT PICTURE LIBRARY

CELTIC PICTURE LIBRARY

THE WALK

ABOVE ABERYSTWYTH

The walk begins at the Tourist Information Centre Ⓐ at the corner of Ffordd y Mor (Terrace Road) and Bath Street, Aberystwyth. There is a car park facing it, while the railway station and bus stops are at the other end of Ffordd y Mor.

1 Go along Ffordd y Mor towards the sea. Turn right along Marine Terrace (becoming Victoria Terrace) to walk with the sea on your left. Go right at the end, towards the Cliff Railway Ⓑ.

2 Just before the Cliff Railway, go left along the zigzag path up Constitution Hill. This is fairly steep but there are benches. Go right over a footbridge across the railway, then left to re-cross it by a second bridge. Reach a café and the Camera Obscura Ⓒ at the top.

3 Go towards the sea and turn right along the cliff-top path (not the broader path inland of it). Walk with a fence on your right and below a radar station.

4 Just before the coastal path goes ahead through conifer trees, turn right over a stile and bear left above the trees. Cross a stile beside a gate on your left to descend along a path through the conifers.

5 Emerge at a hairpin bend in a lane above a caravan site. Fork right uphill to pass a cottage on your right. When the lane bends sharply right uphill, take the waymarked path through the broad-leaved trees ahead. Ignore a path on your right, go ahead to a waymark post and fork left. Pass old stone quarries on your right, ignore a path which forks steeply downhill on your left and go ahead along a path which very gradually descends to a road.

6 Just before the road go sharply right, up a path through the trees. Continue with a hedge on your left and trees on your right to a kissing gate.

7 Go ahead through the kissing gate and with a fence on your left. Cross a stile to the left of a field gate ahead and walk with a fence on your right to a stile ahead. Cross this and veer slightly left across a field between two ruins to a waymarked stile. Go ahead along a fenced track. Ignore the hedged track on your left.

8 Bear left at a fork. Walk with a hedge on your left and a golf course on your right. Pass picnic tables in woodland on your left. You can then stop to admire the view across Aberystwyth to the National Library of Wales Ⓓ. Go ahead down steps and bear right to the road.

9 Go left, then right and left downhill on the road to a junction. Go right down Trefor Road, turn right at North Road, then left down Loveden Road. Veer right across Queen's Road to go up Stryd Portland (Portland Street). This leads to Ffordd y Mor. You can now go right, back to the car park at the start of the walk, or left, to the station and bus stop.

investiture as Prince of Wales. The most eye-catching building is the National Library of Wales Ⓓ. An Englishman, Stuart Rendel, gave the land for it in 1897. This splendid building houses millions of books, maps, pictures and manuscripts, including the 12th-century Welsh *Black Book of Carmarthen*.

A trip to Aberystwyth would not be complete without a ride on the Vale of Rheidol Narrow Gauge

▶ *The coastal path runs along the cliffs between Aberystwyth and Clarach Bay.*

Steam Railway. Opened in 1902 to serve the lead mines, it runs inland for nearly 12 miles (19.2 km) at a gradient of 1:48 to Devil's Bridge. Trains run from the station. This is also the terminus of the standard gauge line from Shrewsbury. The building also houses the Aberystwyth Yesterday Exhibition.

INDEX

Aberystwyth 93–4
Afon Arddu 83, 84
Afon Mynach 89, 92
Alexandra Palace 59–62
almshouses, Heckington 50
Avon, River 73–6

Ballater 15–18
Balmoral Castle 15–18
Bardney Abbey 48
Bardsey Island 93–4
Barney 52
Barrow Hill, Bitton 75
Barton Lane 79, 80
Basford Bridge 36, 37
Bath 73–6
Beacon Hill, Norfolk 53, 55
Beck Hole 23, 24, 25
Beeston Bump 53, 55, 56
Beeston Regis 55, 56
Bell Hotel, Burgh le Marsh 45, 46
Birch Hall Inn 24
Bitton 74, 75
Black Bull Inn 30
Black Lion, Cheddleton 35, 36, 38
Black Watch 16
Boat Inn, Basford Bridge 36
Bodcoll Woollen Mill 92
Bodiam Castle 63–4
Bodley 77, 78
Bodmin and Wadebridge Railway 81–2
Boston, Sleaford and Midland Counties Railway
    49
Bran Point 70, 71
brass industry 73, 75
Bratoft 45
Bretts Farm 57, 58
Bridgnorth 39–42
Bron-y-Buckley Wood 86, 87
Brontë Falls 30, 32
Brontë Parsonage Museum 30
Brontë sisters 29, 32
Burgh le Marsh 43–6
burial mounds 45, 75
Buttington Wharf 86, 87

Caethro 86, 87
Caldon Canal 35, 36, 37
Caldy Hill 33, 34
Camel Valley 81–2
camera obscura, Aberystwyth 93, 94
canals
    Caldon 35, 36, 37
    Car Dyke 48–9
    Kennet and Avon 73
    Montgomeryshire 85, 86, 87
Car Dyke 48–9
Cartway, Bridgnorth 40, 41
castles
    Balmoral 15–18
    Bodiam 63–4
    Bridgenorth 41, 42
    Holwell 78
    Muncaster 19–20
    Powis 85, 86, 88
Cawdron, Robert 48, 49
Ceredigion Museum 93
Ceunant Mawr waterfall 83, 84
Chappel 57–8

Cheddleton 35–8
Christ Church 86, 87, 88
Church House, Heckington 50
Churchtown 77–8
Churnet, River 35–8
Clarach, River 93
Cleveland Way 27, 28
cliff railways
    Aberystwyth 93–4
    Bridgnorth 39, 40–1, 42
Cloughton 27, 28
coastal walks
    Aberystwyth 93–4
    Dawlish 79–80
    north Norfolk 56
    Osmington 69–72
    Scarborough 27
Cock Hill 45
Coed Rheidol 90
Coed-y-wlad 87
Colne, River 57–8
Consall 36–8
Constitution Hill, Aberystwyth 93
Coryton's Cove 79, 80
Cottage Loaf, Thurstaston 33, 34
country parks
    Penistone Hill 32
    Wirral 33–4
Craigendarroch 16, 17
Craven Heifer, Stainforth 21
Crawfish Inn 51, 52
Crouch Hill Station 60
Crown Inn, Eardington 39

Daniel's Mill 39, 40, 41–2
Darnholme 25
Dawlish 79–80
Dee, River 15–18, 33–4
Deeside Railway 16, 18
Devil's Bridge, Dyfed 89–92
Devil's Punchbowl 89, 92
Dinas Ty-du 84
disused railways
    Bitton to Bath 73, 74–5, 76
    Bodmin and Wadebridge Railway 81–2
    Camel Trail 81–2
    East Lincolnshire 46
    Finsbury Park 59–62
    Hooton to West Kirby 33
    Lambourn Valley Railway 68
    Parkland Walk 59–62
    Scarborough to Whitby 27
    Severn Valley line 39, 42
    Welshpool and Llanfair Light Railway 85, 86,
        87
    Whitby to Pickering 23–4, 26
Dorset Coast Path 69
Downs 66

Eardington 39–42
East Anglian Railway museum 57
East Garston 65–8
East Lincolnshire Railway 46
East Runton 54
Eastbury 65–8
Eller Beck Valley 25
Empson's Hill 79, 80
Esk, River 19
Ewhurst Green 64

Fairview 77, 78
Fenland, Heckington 47–50
Finsbury Park, London 59–62
fishing, Norfolk 56
Fleece Inn, Burgh le Marsh 45
Flint Mill 36, 37, 38
flint pebbles 56, 65
Fordstreet 57, 58
Frankton Junction 87
Froghall 37, 38
Fylingdales Early Warning Station 26

Gairn, Bridge of 16, 17
Gallowstree Bank 86, 87
Glannoventa 20
Glengairn Church 16, 17
Glenmuick Church 16, 17
Goathland 23–7
Golden Line 27
Grace Evans Cottage 87, 88
Granary Steps, Bridgnorth 41
Great Hale 48, 49
Great Northern Railway 49
Great Western Railway 68, 76
Green Park station, Bath 76
green ways, Bodley 77, 78
Grosmont 26
Gunby Hall 43, 46

Hafod Arms 89, 90
hares 65, 67
Haworth 29–32
Heckington 47–50
Heddon House 77
Heddon Valley 78
Helland 81–2
Hellandbridge 81
Highgate Wood 59, 61–2
hillforts 84, 93
Hoffmann kiln 22
Holden Park 31, 32
Holwell Castle 78
Hooton to West Kirby railway 33
horse racing 65–8
Hundale Point 27

Iron industry 24, 38, 41
Irt, River 19

Keighley and Worth Valley Railway 32
Kennet and Avon canal 73
Kent and East Sussex railway 64
Keynsham 73–6
Killington 78
kilns 21, 22, 35, 37–8

Lambourn Valley 65–8
Lambourn Valley Railway 68
Langcliffe Quarry 22
Langstone Rock 80
Lavington's Hole 40, 41
Lea Mount 79, 80
lead mines 89, 90, 91
Lilla Cross 26
Lincolnshire Railway Museum 46
Lindsey Marsh 43–6
'Little Ratt' 19
Llanberis 83–4
Llanfair Caereinion 87

Lleyn Peninsula 93–4
Llyn Padarn 83, 84
Lochnagar 18
Locks 22
London, Parkland Walk 59–62
long-distance paths 27, 28, 69, 79
Lower Kernick 82
Lynton and Barnstaple railway 77

Mallyan Spout 23–4
Manor Farm 65, 66
marshes 43–6, 47–50
Mill Scar 25
mills
 Avon mill 73
 Bodcoll Woollen Mill 90, 92
 Burgh le Marsh 45
 Daniel's Mill 39, 40, 41–2
 Flint 36, 37, 38
 the Mill in the Hole 42
 Muncaster 20
 Vale Mill 32
Mite, River 19, 20
model railways 77, 78
Montgomeryshire canal 85, 86, 87
moorland 23–7, 29–32
mountain railways, Snowdon 83–4
Muncaster Castle 19, 20
Muncaster Mill 19, 20
museums
 Brontë Parsonage 30
 Ceredigion 93
 East Anglian Railway 57
 Lincolnshire Railway Museum 46
 Powysland 85, 86
 Sheringham 56
Muswell Hill 61, 62

Nag's Head 49
narrow-gauge railways
 Lynton and Barnstaple 77, 78
 Ravenglass and Eskdale 19–20
 Thursford 51
 Vale of Rheidol 89, 90, 94
national parks 23–7
nature reserves 37, 38, 90–1
North Norfolk Railway 53, 56
North Staffordshire Railway 37
North York Moors National Park 23–7
North Yorkshire Moors Railway 23, 25
Northgate, Bridgnorth 39, 41

Oakmeadow Ford Lock 36, 37
Oakworth Station 31, 32
Old Crawfish Forge 51, 52
Orby 45–6
Osmington 69–72
Osmington Mills 70, 72

Parkland Walk, North London 59–62
Parracombe 77–8
Parson's Bridge 90, 91
Pearoom Craft Centre 47
Pen Dinas 93
Penglais Woods 93
Penistone Hill 30, 31–2
Pennington Arms Hotel 19
Pixon Barn 70, 71, 72
Poppy Line 53

Potseething Spring 40, 42
Powis Castle 85, 86, 88
Powysland museum 85, 86
Pretty Corner, Norfolk 53–6

Queen's Wood, London 59, 61

Racehorses 65–8
Railway Hotel, Heckington 49
raines 21
Ratty Arms 19
Ravenglass 19–20
Ravenglass and Eskdale Railway 19, 20
Red Lion, Orby 43, 45
Rheidol, Vale of 89–92
Ribble, River 21–2
Roman remains
 Ravenglass 19, 20
 Roman Camp, Norfolk 53–6
Rother, River 63–4
Royal Bridge, Ballater 17
Runton 53–6

St Andrew's Church, Heckington 48, 50
St Andrew's Church, Thursford 52
St Barnabas Church, Chappel 57
St James's Lane 62
St John's Church, Ysbyty Cynfyn 90, 92
St Laurence, Church of 27, 28
St Leonard's Church, Bridgnorth 40–1
St Mary's Church, Barney 52
St Mary's Church, Goathland 23
St Mary's Church, Welshpool 86
St Mungo's Well 17
St Peter and St Paul, Church of 45
St Petrock's Church, Parracombe 77–8
Salden Beck 32
Saltford 74, 75
Scalby 27–8
Scarborough 27
Scarborough to Whitby railway 27
sculpture trail 75, 76
Settle–Carlisle Railway 21
Severn, River, Bridgnorth 39–42
Severn Valley Line 39, 42
shannocks 56
sheep 21, 23
Shell Wood 82
Sheringham 53, 56
Shoulder of Mutton pub 57, 58
Skelton, Tom 20
smugglers 72, 80
Smuggler's Inn, Osmington 69–72
Snagshall 64
Snowdon 83–4
South Devon Railway 79
South West Coastal Path 79
Stainforth 21–2
Stanbury 30, 32
steam engines, Thursford 51–2
steam trains
 Bitton 74, 75, 76
 Bridgenorth–Kidderminster 41–2
 East Anglian Railway 57–8
 East Lincolnshire Railway 46
 Keighley and Worth Valley 32
 Kent and East Sussex line 64
 North Norfolk Railway 53, 56
 North Staffordshire Railway 37

North Yorkshire Moors 23, 25, 26
 Ravenglass and Eskdale 19, 20
 Settle–Carlisle Railway 21
 The Poppy Line 53
 Vale of Rheidol Railway 89, 90, 94
 Welshpool and Llanfair Light Railway 86, 87
stone circles, Temple Cairn 90, 91
Stoneway Steps 41, 42
strip lynchets 72
Stroud Green Station 60
Strumble Head 93–4
Sunray pub 69, 70
Swineford 74

Temple Cairn Circle 90, 91
Thomason Foss 25
Thursford 51–2
Thurstaston Common 34
Thurstaston Hill 33–4
Top Withens 29, 32

Udiam 64
Upper Ladypark Wood 38
Upper Sheringham 55
Upton Brook 70

Vale Mill 32
Vale of Rheidol Railway 89, 90, 94
Victoria, Queen 15–18

Wakes Colne 57–8
Water Ark Foss 25
weaving, Haworth 29, 31, 32
Welshpool 85–8
Welshpool and Llanfair Light Railway 85, 86, 87
West Beck 23
West Kirby 33
West Runton 53, 55
Whitby to Pickering Railway 23–4, 26
white horse, Osmington 70, 71, 72
White Swan, Burgh le Marsh 44, 45
windmills
 Burgh le Marsh 45, 46
 Heckington 47, 48, 50
Winterdown Bottom 66
Wirral Way 33–4
wreckers 72, 80

Ysbyty Cynfyn church 90, 92

Index compiled by INDEXING SPECIALISTS, Hove.